MY SON MY HERO A MOTHERS JOURNAL

MY SON MY HERO A MOTHERS JOURNAL

✦

Sergeant First Class Paul R. Smith
MEDAL OF HONOR WAR ON TERRORISM

J.P.

iUniverse, Inc.
New York Lincoln Shanghai

MY SON MY HERO A MOTHERS JOURNAL
Sergeant First Class Paul R. Smith MEDAL OF HONOR WAR ON TERRORISM

Copyright © 2005 by JANICE PVIRRE

iUniverse books may be ordered through booksellers or by contacting:

iUniverse
2021 Pine Lake Road, Suite 100
Lincoln, NE 68512
www.iuniverse.com
1-800-Authors (1-800-288-4677)

ISBN-13: 978-0-595-37085-6 (pbk)
ISBN-13: 978-0-595-67457-2 (cloth)
ISBN-13: 978-0-595-81485-5 (ebk)
ISBN-10: 0-595-37085-3 (pbk)
ISBN-10: 0-595-67457-7 (cloth)
ISBN-10: 0-595-81485-9 (ebk)

Printed in the United States of America

To my son, Paul Ray Smith, who gave me joy, laughter, and love; a boy who taught me lessons in life as well as in his death.

Dedicated to my son, my hero, my family, and to all the parents of fallen heroes.

To my son's "boys," who shared my grief.

To all of our troops, who fight for our freedom every single day.

From the thoughts, memories and the tears of a mother's heart, I pledge to you my deepest gratitude and acknowledgement.

Contents

Acknowledgments

All glory goes to the Lord for trusting me with His most precious gift, His son and mine. Without His mercy, love and grace this book would never have been written.

To my wonderful husband, who traveled down dark paths with me; who loved and encouraged me every step of my journey.

To my wonderful children, who contributed stories that I had never heard until Paul's death.

To my friend, my rock in the storm who stood by me all the way, my sister Sharon Cate.

To the boys that my son loved, who shared my grief.

To my sister-in-law, Barbara Freeman, who said I could do this.

To the military for recognizing a real hero.

For all the parents that have lost a child in this war. Life has changed forever, but as they would want us to, we will continue on.

To Rusty Fischer, my editor, who put the polish on this manuscript with his compassion and knowledge. He was my angel sent from God and I will be forever grateful for his help.

To Alex Leary, writer for the St. Petersburg newspaper who brought my son's story to the public—and to the newspaper for starting a web site in honor of my son.

Authors Note

✦

A Mother's Healing Process

To date there have been over 1,836 deaths as a result of the war in Iraq. That means that there are now over 1,836 parents trying to deal with the loss of a child. I am one of those parents; this is my journey.

When my father died, I was in my twenties with two children to care for. At the time, I had no concept of how to grieve. Therefore, I was a very angry young woman for many years until, at some point, missing my father simply became a part of my life. I know that the extreme pain I felt all those years held me back from being the person that he would have encouraged me to be.

April 4, 2003. This is the day that shattered my life in two; this is the day that my son, Paul Ray Smith, was killed just outside of the Baghdad International Airport in Iraq. He was there doing a job that he loved; a job that he believed in.

He was there because he knew the cost of freedom.

He paid it in full that day.

I am forever in his debt…

This book did not start out to be a published work. I never imagined it having a cover and being read by anyone other than myself. In fact, I started this journal because I missed my beloved son so much that I thought that if I talked to him every day in the pages of this journal, I could somehow be closer to him. Without my being aware of the different steps of grieving that exist, this journal walked me through the healing process—step-by-step—without me even knowing it.

It is only with the grace and mercy of the Lord that I have finished this book and now would like to share with other parents how I was able to wake up in the morning and get out of bed and…just…*breathe.*

When we lose a child, there is a beginning and an end; then there is another beginning and, eventually, another end. When we have our children and go through this busy life of raising them, we don't ever consider that we will have to bury them; this is in no way a part of our plans for their lives. But, alas, this *does* happen and when it does this is the end of our own lives, or so we feel at the time.

We bury our child and try to go on; we go through the motions and try to act "normal" so our family and friends don't worry about us too much. Life splits in two: there is a time before death and then, after death, a new life to begin without this person in it.

I hope to share with my readers the different emotions that I have lived with for the past two years. This included unbearable pain that I knew I would never live without, depression so deep that it kept me from living in the here and now, despair and longing for a different end to this story, and anger that I didn't think could ever *not* be a part of my life.

It was when I finally acknowledged that Paul's physical presence in my life was at an end that the healing process finally began. In this journal I was able to explore all the aspects of my life with my son and even surprised myself with the knowledge that it brought forth. I have learned how to celebrate the man that he was and be grateful for the time I spent with him.

I hope that this book will help other parents that have lost a son or daughter in war. I realize that our lives have been altered for all time, but our lives have not ended—as I often thought mine would. We do go on a little stronger and a little braver for what we have experienced. If our grieving process is complete we will carry on as our children would want us to; we will celebrate life in their honor.

In the end, I suppose, that is their final gift to us...

About the Book

✦

My Son; My Hero

This journal is one mother's two-year journey after her son died in the hot dessert of Iraq, were the sand drank his blood and cost an entire family their loved one's legacy.

This book will take the reader to cities all across the country for recognitions her son received for his valor. You will accompany her to New York City to ground zero, where it all began. You will travel with her to a building in Orlando, Florida and see a structure that now wears his name—and face. You will visit the warm waters of the Gulf-of-Mexico, were she says her last good-bye to her beloved son.

This is a journey that took her all the way to the Pentagon, to The Hall of Heroes, to the White House to meet the man that sent her son to war, and finally to the hallowed grounds of Arlington Cemetery.

The reader will travel with her down the long road of grief and sadness. You will feel the extreme joy with which this beloved child filled her life. You will feel the anger and experience the pain in her heart, as she shares with you feelings never expressed before.

This journal is about an ordinary boy from south Tampa, Florida who became an extraordinary man in a war-torn region halfway across the globe.

The journal will have readers swelling with pride to know that someone loved them enough to die for their freedom; to allow them to wake up every morning and know that they are free and to remember that freedom, in fact, is *never* free. This is the story of one mother's journey toward finding closure with her son's death.

This is one mother's journal…

Prologue

◆

April 4, 2003

Spring had already faded into warm summer days in our southeastern town of Holiday, Florida. The seasons passed without notice, without celebration, without anything more than the turning pages of a calendar and the sudden realization that our former favorite TV shows were suddenly in reruns.

We weren't watching them anyway. The war in Iraq had started and like most families with loved ones "over there," life suddenly consisted of a television screen, endless hours of praying, and the constant waiting that has been both blessing and curse to generations of military families.

From the mothers who pined over their lost boys during the American Revolution and later the Civil War to those who watched their young boys go off to fight World Wars I and II to those of us who watched every night on CNN for a glimpse of our own sons, now fighting the dirtier, longer wars against terrorism and the ever-elusive Weapons of Mass Destruction, the feeling was quite the same: days without number, nights without end.

These days, which were no different from when Paul left to answer the call of duty, as with so many other duty assignments, we waited. We called each other daily to see if anyone had heard from him in the desert, hoping in vain for any bit of information that might have been an answer to our prayers.

Today was no different. The house was quiet; the television had been on twenty-four hours a day since the war started. We no longer bothered with local channels or cable; our set was dutifully tuned in to CNN in order to get the latest news from the Middle East.

It was no exaggeration to claim that I had literally become a prisoner to my television, afraid to leave the house lest I miss seeing a glimpse of Paul on the screen. CNN was live in Iraq and I knew that if I watched long enough I would see Paul and know that he was safe—for the moment.

I never did see him.

As April 3rd bled into April 4th, I spent another endless evening watching the war on CNN, hoping and praying for just a small glimpse of his face. It was like a running loop, featuring the same familiar commentators, the same dusty hair, the same awkward pauses as news was beamed halfway around the world.

I quickly got used to the running ticker tape at the bottom of the screen, blaring its endless stream of facts, figures, and statistics as if to underscore the images of explosion, boredom, and bravery nightly featured on the screen. I watched without seeing, listened without hearing, often looking up to see that minutes, sometimes even hours, had passed without a single image or sound-bite registering.

That night was the same as any other night. I turned the TV off, said my prayers—prayers for his safety, prayers for other families who had loved ones in harm's way, prayers for a quick resolution to this global conflict, prayers for our President—but that night I was more restless then on most nights.

Sleep came slowly, as it had on most nights since the war started. Little did I know that when sleep ended that night, my own personal war was just beginning...

12:30 a.m.

In the black of night the phone started to ring. There was no flicking on of the light switch or fumbling around for glasses, like you see on TV or in the movies; before the first ring stopped I had the receiver in my hand and was sputtering a frenzied, "Hello?!?" In a split second my mind screamed that a middle of the night call had to be bad news; already my stomach was turning over and tying into knots.

On the other end of the line an awkward silence was interrupted by an anguished cry...

1

The Call Every Mother Dreads

A tiny muffled cry that was almost inaudible announced without preamble, "Daddy's died."

"Jessie, is this you?" I managed to croak into the phone.

Again the voice cried out over the telephone wires, "Daddy's died!"

I didn't have to pinch myself to know this was not a dream...

In the background I could hear my daughter-in-law, Birgit, moaning, crying, wailing painful screams and disbelief, all of which were echoed in my granddaughter's pitiful little voice. "Grandma, Daddy's died."

"Jessica," I replied forcefully, "tell Mom I'm on my way. I'll be there by sunup."

My husband, Don, lay next to me in the bed, half-awake and only semiconscious; he asked who was on the phone. "Don," I replied, "wake up, that was Jessica. Paul's died and I have to leave."

It was a before and after moment; forevermore life would be divided into what our family was like before that fateful phone call, and how we coped afterward. There was no time for regret or sorrow; there was only time for action.

With no other information at all I started to move but had no idea what to do first. I knew what I wanted to do first: I wanted a cigarette. I had quit smoking over a year earlier but I needed one right then, right at that very moment. Somehow, I avoided the temptation.

I don't remember what was said or what I was thinking; all I knew was that I had to be with Birgit and my two grandchildren. I don't even think that my mind was registering the fact that my son had been killed yet; if it had, I'm sure I would have slumped to the floor and stayed there for days. Instead, instinct took over and my body just kept moving on automatic pilot.

Meanwhile, Don called my sister Sharon to see if she would accompany me for the five-hour ride to Fort Stewart, Georgia. I knew he was worried about me driving alone, but at the time he was unable to make the drive with me due to recent surgery.

I pulled a suitcase from the closet and hastily packed it with items unknown at the time. I figured that if I needed anything when I got there I would buy it in Georgia. Normally I'd be packed days in advance if I knew I was going to visit my son; this wasn't that type of trip.

I don't remember the drive to my sister's house to pick her up, nor do I remember crying or having any thoughts in my mind at all. At the time I was only aware of the movement of my body. My body was numb, as if frozen from being out in the cold for too long.

The five-hour drive from Holiday, Florida to Hinesville, Georgia, where Paul had been stationed at Fort Stewart for the past few years, was mostly silent; if we talked at all I don't remember what was said. I do remember the darkness of the night and the fact that, mercifully, there were not many other drivers on the road.

My big Lincoln seemed cold, even in April, when the weather was normally very pleasant; for the most part, the drive was smooth and quiet. Was the radio playing? If it was, I surely don't remember. As I touched the steering wheel I felt as if I was not driving at all but just sitting there behind the wheel. I might as well have been sitting on the couch in my living room. Even with my sister right there by my side I felt alone and very, very lonely.

The temptation was strong and I had succumbed. As soon as I left the house I bought my first pack of cigarettes in years and started right up where I left off. As I drove I continued to chain smoke and not remember the little towns I went through. I had no details of the situation, no time frame, and no information at all; I only knew I had to be there with my family no matter what the situation.

The drive was surreal; I often felt like my body wasn't even in the car but far away, just drifting along with the movement. I continued to drive, not remembering when we stopped for gas or if we even talked. I'm sure we did but nothing seemed to be registering. Once in a while my sister would remind me of my speed in a so gentle voice, as if she was whispering to me.

As I drove my mind naturally went back in time to the picture in my head of a fair-haired, blue-green eyed child, one-and-a-half years old sitting in a high chair chewing on a barbecued rib, covered in barbecue sauce from his eyebrows to his tiny little pink toes. The year was 1971 and we were still living in El Paso, Texas, were Paul Ray was born.

Such a sight he was; his little angelic face so sleepy from a day of play and needing nothing more than what is needed at that age: love, food, and protection, all of which he had in abundance.

As I drove up highway I-75 toward my destination other pictures of Paul Ray ran through my mind like frames in a slide projector. A few times I would find myself with tears in my eyes, the road becoming blurry and unsafe in my field of unsure vision, and I would have to remind myself that I had to drive; there would be time for tears later.

Meanwhile I continued to drive and the slide projector continued to show me pictures in my mind: Three years old, walking and taking, blue-green eyes always smiling at me with a look of knowledge, even at his young age. I always said that Paul had an "old soul." This was the first of many moves for little Paul. A new home in a new country and for me a new baby on the way in the fall. Paul Ray's little body constantly in motion and the words becoming so much clearer and talking all the time, always wanting new information or explanations of "why, why Mom," always "why."

Paul was always a happy boy, not needing much attention or new toys to play with at this age. His greatest joy on that day was sitting in a huge moving box with packing peanuts stuck to every inch of his little body, thanks to a big, red, sticky sucker that he slowly licked away.

An hour before his naptime we would get all bundled up against the cold and go outside to get fresh air; this was our special playtime. We would go out to find adventures in this vast New World, and no matter what we did—or didn't—find, it was always an adventure for him. Little Paul could pick up a rock and examine it for a long time until he had decided that he had looked at every angle of the rock, satisfied and approved of it. Then he would softly lay it on the ground so he wouldn't damage it. Even at this early age he was a gentle boy.

Often he would chase a butterfly and when it landed on a surface that Paul could see he would be afraid to touch it, but always wanted to look closely. Then came nap time and I would go in and look at him in slumber and think, "How could that sweet little guy have come from me?"

I always felt so blessed when I would look in at my children as they slept so peacefully; in my mind's eye I could always see them wrapped in soft white angel wings and when they were awake I marveled at the way they learned new things. Above all it taught me a valuable lesson; one that came in handy as I drove that fateful night: Children are truly gifts from God and need to be cherished every day.

My little guy turned four-and-a-half before I realized how fast he was growing. Now he was playing and making Army wars in a big round hole in the backyard where an above ground pool once stood. Little green Army men were always one of his favorite things to play with. Today, thinking back and seeing him play war with those little toys, I wonder if he had any idea of his own destiny, or if it was just a game to him, a game that most little boys played like cowboys and Indians.

A move back to the states, a new house, and soon he would be going to school. I will never forget Paul's first day of school; my mental slide show revealed a little man going off that first day, not a little boy. I remember that he didn't want me to walk him, he was too big for that now and the school was only two blocks away. As he assured me he would be fine, he further promised me he would do everything right, just like I told him. I watched as my little boy was off for his next new adventure, all dressed up in new clothes and a lunch pail that held his favorite snack, so excited, so happy and I knew that this was the beginning of his growing up.

How easily Paul always adapted to new places and new people; he hated moving all the time and having to say good-bye to friends but he never complained. Even then he was a real trooper. He was just a happy, ordinary little boy, with new friends to make and new adventures awaiting him there in our new home in the warm Florida Keys.

The road unwound before me.

My slide show continued...

Finding Treasures—and Trouble—on the Beach

Screams of pain rang in my ears and, tracking its all-too-familiar source, I found Paul and his little sister lying in the sand; they had found a group of jelly-fish on the beach and proceeded to bombard them with rocks, creating an unpleasant side effect: The stinging agent had splashed back on their arms and legs; already a rash was starting to hurt, turning an angry red. A run to the hospital for treatment and all was well for another day, but for my two curious kids it was a lesson not soon forgotten.

Long days spent on the beach turned Paul's skin the color of a copper penny and his hair an even lighter shade of blonde. How much like the all American boy he looked; how young and full of life. We spent our days combing the beach, collecting anything and everything—and avoiding anymore jellyfish! Every new shell was another something to drag home and save; haphazard souvenirs from the endless adventures always waiting just around the corner for this curious little boy.

Around the age of ten, Paul Ray's personality had started to develop at an accelerated pace; I saw so many different sides of him coming into view. There was the "funny" side of Paul; locking his baby sister in an oversized rabbit cage for the fun of it and leaving her there till I came home from work; at least *he* thought it was funny.

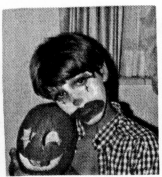

Then there was the very kind side of Paul; offering me his piece of pie because there were only four pieces and five of us. (I finally convinced him that I didn't want it and he should eat it now before one of his siblings could see it and devour it.) As he sat eating his pie I would give him a smile and he would give me a little wink. 'Nuff said. It was like that with us; sometimes he wouldn't have to talk to speak volumes, but his smile would always say, "Thanks Mom, I love you."

Paul and I seemed to speak to each other without having to say a word; it was like we spoke a silent language to each other. Around this age Paul became very melodramatic; a slight accident became a major event. I think it was because I often worked several jobs and we didn't always have a lot of time together.

I think he needed more attention then I could give him at that time. Today I wish I would have taken more time to share the little things with him; the quiet moments between mother and son: the homework and the backyard ballgames and the TV shows and coloring books and the simple desserts I missed simply because I was too busy when I came home from work to enjoy them together.

What in our busy life could have been more important than my children? But hindsight is always 20/20 and these are but lessons learned far too late. How this kid turned out as good as he did I can only say that it was the Lord looking out for His beloved son.

They say necessity is the mother of all invention and perhaps it was because of my absence around the house that it was around this time that Paul found his first very best friend for life. Greg Harris lived in our new neighborhood and soon became Paul's shadow. I loved watching them together; they were more like brothers than friends. Paul was tall and skinny, Greg shorter and a little plump, but they were always together nonetheless.

The slide show continued with pictures of Paul and, as always, Greg right there at his side. My mind recalls the parade of broken bones, scrapes and bruises from a typical American boyhood. A discarded hub cap along the road became a ring on Paul's middle finger that got stuck and we couldn't get off; another trip to the hospital emergency room and soon that hub cap became a part of Paul's never ending collection of everything he'd ever seen, experienced, or collected.

Paul Ray was a quiet kid but he spoke volumes with his eyes and expressions. Firm in his convictions, he rarely got fighting mad but when the time was right you knew were he stood on any matter, be it earth shattering or insignificant. He was a born pack rat; everything had a value to this curious little guy and he knew if he kept the item long enough he would find a use for it "one day."

There was not a radio in the house that Paul did not take apart at one time or another and put back together with always a few parts left over, in spite of that fact the radio always worked. He was a wizard of technology, and treated his own life much the way he treated old radios or hubcaps; he was a collector of experiences as much as he was of "things."

The slide show ratcheted up a notch, revealing: Bike tricks, camping in the woods, borrowing Mom's car without permission, getting stopped by the police after a car chase—with the car ending up in a ditch! Playing with fireworks on the Fourth of July after being told he couldn't, and in general being an ordinary boy that surely added more gray hair to my head each day.

With Paul there was always laughter, that wonderful laugh of his, each tone meant something different. There was the one that was so hard it brought tears to his eyes, and another one that meant, "Hey, I got you this time." There was one laugh that said, "You don't know everything" and another that touted his sister by bragging without saying a word but always accompanied by that silly sideways smirk, "I know a secret and I'm not going to tell you."

Paul's smile also had hidden meanings, and he knew how to use it. The soft smile that said, "I'm sorry Mom," the sly smirk that let him get away with just about anything and the smile that just plain warmed your heart. No matter what kind of a smile it was, it was always there, ready, open, and willing to share and always given away freely; no price for admission.

His smile earned him lasting friendships: Even after we moved to a different house and neighborhood, Paul was in a different school but Greg was always there, a part of our lives as he continues to be even to this day.

There was a kindness in Paul's heart that you didn't see in most kids his age. It was sincere, compassionate, and always willing to help those that needed it. Like helping the older woman next door carry in her groceries even when he and Greg were in the middle of playing some game or another. Stopping and helping never seemed be a question; he just did it. He would stop to help another kid that was being harassed, going the extra mile for a friend even though he knew he was going to get in trouble for it.

It was a kind of compassion that seemed strange for a kid his age, and warred with the funny, wisecracking Paul that was always pulling pranks on everyone. Paul was fun to be with; he laughed easily and always wore that great smile, so warm, inviting and caring.

High school came; suddenly my precious little boy had turned into a strapping young man who was tall, tan, slight and good looking. Other changes were in the air. Now, too, life was taking on a different light.

There was the future to consider…

Paul became a carpenter's assistant while in high school, so I thought that this would be his life's work because he was so good at it but, most of all, because he just plain liked it.

Thinking back I can always remember that whenever you asked Paul what he wanted to be when he grew up, even from an early age, his answer was always the same; it never faltered, never changed. He would always simply say, "I plan to go into the Army and have a family..."

At the time, that answer seemed so simple for a kid...

To the Graduate
June 1989

Graduation pictures ran through my mind next. How proud he was to be the first one of his siblings to graduate from high school and, as always, there was Greg standing by his side to cheer him on. That year I didn't have the money to buy him something nice for his graduation so I wrote him a letter instead.

It read simply:

My darling Paul,

When first I saw you so very small and needing, I knew you were a gift from God, one that He entrusted me with. God gave me the knowledge to be your protector, your teacher, your safe place to fall whenever you needed to.

When you were but a toddler God gave me strong shoulders not only to carry your slight frame but also to carry all your hurt and pain.

God gave me His loving hands to guide you down the path of this life that wasn't always smooth or easy for you; it was He who held your hand.

My knowledge of right and wrong and good and bad came from Him so I could lead you. Sometimes I wondered if it was real, but seldom questioned His knowledge because you always proved it to be right.

For nineteen years I have cared for God's gift to this world and now the world is ready for the most perfect you.

Paul, there are no words for me to write that could tell you how proud I am of you; the pride fills my heart till I feel it will surely burst.

In the Bible it says that God created man in His image to walk this earth and share the knowledge of His love. I see you sharing this knowledge and love with those you come in contact with everyday and again I am so proud of you.

Paul, I could not have done such a good job of raising you without the Lord. I was but His instructor and you His perfect student that He entrusted with me.

You have never failed to be all that I knew you could be, and I thank God everyday that He gave you to me, if only for a short time.

Your values in life and your moral strengths will pave your path through life. Don't allow anyone to change your morals and I promise you, you will accomplish great things in your lifetime. You are chosen to do great things.

Always,

Your friend and mother

Even then I seemed to have known that God had something great planned for my Paul.

After high school, the picture in my mind of Paul was like a defining moment in all of our lives: A tall, lanky, good-looking suntanned young boy in a white T-shirt with the sleeves slightly rolled and torn blue jeans at the knees rode up into our driveway on his motorcycle. As soon as I saw him that fateful day I knew by the look in those beautiful blue-green eyes he had something important on his mind to tell us.

After a warm greeting, we went out back to sit facing the pond behind our house. As a soft breeze ruffled his sun-bleached hair I watched his eyes even as he continued to wipe the sweat off the tall glass of iced tea he was holding.

It reminded me of a time on the beach in Key West when he looked the same while he was trying to decide whether or not he wanted to tell me he had done something bad. The wind had blown his hair the same way that day. I could tell he was trying to pick the perfect moment to tell us his "big news." As he finally looked up into my eyes I knew this really *was* something big.

The world seemed to quiet a little and then, proudly with a smile as big as Texas, he announced that he had joined the Army and would be leaving for Fort Leonard Wood in Missouri for basic training.

The next day...

I didn't know what he was expecting to see on my face, but his eyes had that look in them when he would be silently begging me for something that he wasn't sure I would give. He was waiting for me to say something, and all I could think of at that precise moment was how beautiful he was and how much I loved him.

That, and how much our lives would be changed forever as a result of what he'd just told us. He waited patiently for me to react and, when I finally did, I had to admit that my emotions were mixed. On one hand I was sad because he would be leaving us to start a new chapter in his life, but on the other hand I was happy for him because he was doing exactly what he always said he wanted to do.

That day, looking into his face, I never thought of the "what ifs..."

The very last picture I have of my little boy was of him putting on his helmet and waving goodbye with a smile that told me he would be just fine; I never saw that same smile ever again.

That evening as I sat and held Paul's Manx cat, Sassy Cat, I knew that Sassy would live with us for the rest of his life. As I sat with tears in my heart I knew that my little boy was going to be a man very soon; that a new chapter was about to begin.

Basic Training

Letters soon started coming from Fort Leonard Wood, saying that basic was hard and how he missed us all, but most of all he missed the good food that he left behind. Soon followed a letter telling me how much trouble he got into for having bought and brought a very large bag of his favorite candy, M&Ms, into the barracks, and the punishment he'd received for the deed when he was finally caught. The envelope that contained that letter had a stick figure being hung with a noose and little round M&Ms drawn all over it.

On another envelope he had drawn crude pictures of Army trucks, guns and Army boots. To this day I have envelopes that have funny pictures drawn on them that you would have thought a very small child had made. I'm here to tell you that my boy had absolutely no talent for drawing. Nonetheless, every envelope saved is a treasure to me; as I look at them now they remind me of how happy he really was, and I smile under the coat of tears that threatens to drown out their vision.

My oldest daughter, Lisa, and I flew to Missouri to see Paul graduate from basic. Leave it to a mother to embarrass her son the day before graduation. As my daughter and I pulled into the gates of the base a soft and slow rain had started and it was cold. The gate guard told us where to go to find Paul; we proceeded onto base as instructed but could not find the location of Paul's barracks so we stopped at another building and again were told where to find him. Before we got to the right barracks Paul's First Sergeant had already called ahead to say that "Paul's mommy was looking for him."

Needless to say it was announced over the PA system for all to hear. I felt so bad for him but as always Paul just smiled and said it was "no big deal." I tried to believe him but in my heart of hearts, I was sure he must have gotten a lot of good-natured ribbing over that one.

As instructed, Lisa and I waited outside for Paul next to our rented car. The slight mist that continued to fall was refreshing because I was so nervous and so excited about seeing him. Soon a group of guys all in green and all looking like each other appeared from around the end of the building. At first I didn't see him. To be honest, I think in my mind I was looking for my little boy and here standing in front of me was a stranger with my son's smile.

The hugs and kisses we exchanged that day were the best I had in so very long. We were only allowed a few hours with Paul before he had to return to the barracks and us to our hotel; tomorrow would be graduation day. After graduation

Lisa and I wanted to take Paul for the day into St. Louis to the zoo and just spend the day with him; we were so excited and happy to be with him.

Another defining picture in my collection on my silent side projector.

How beautiful and proud he was. I will never forget the proud look on his face that said, "Look at me, Mom. I did it!" I was certain that his uniform buttons were going to pop off with the swelling pride in his chest. I took a picture of the pride he wore that day and even now I can't help but smile when I look at it.

That picture has always been one of my favorites and has always hung over my desk, where I still talk to him every day. After graduation Paul told us that he would be leaving for his first assignment, Germany, and would not have any time to spend with us. It was our first experiment with that most onerous of military terms: orders! We had so little time with him but believe you me every second was cherished. This new chapter of his life was underway and he was so happy.

How could we begrudge him that?

First Assignment:
Germany

In a new country, seeing new things, Paul flourished, writing home often about long training in the field. Training that he thought would never end and was sure that it would kill him or at least leave him scarred for life. Reading over his letters, it was clear that although he'd become a man my little boy hadn't changed all that much after all; he still had a rather melodramatic air about him.

The training didn't kill him; instead it invigorated him. Soon came fewer letters home. Suddenly he was too busy seeing the country, partying with new friends, a lot of training, a new girl in his life and more important things to do besides writing home.

I *did* understand, but that didn't mean I had to like it...

And Now, Desert Storm

His first war, and now I think of "the what ifs…"

2

Arriving

The sun was coming up and I knew I was getting close to Fort Stewart—and the truth. The closer I got to Paul and Birgit's house, the more fear was setting into my weary bones.

I didn't want to know the truth. I wanted to go home and watch CNN and hope I would see my son's face. I wanted to wait for this war to be over so Paul Ray could come home. I didn't want this to be true. I wanted this to be a bad dream and I would soon wake up, turn on the television, pour my first cup of coffee, and listen to the birds that serenaded me every morning.

I wanted to just sit and watch the news.

Was that so horrible?

As I drove into the cul-de-sac outside of Paul and Birgit's house I saw Lisa, our daughter, standing there waiting for me. As if she knew I'd be there any minute. As if she sensed the car pulling up the road.

That was the moment I knew it was so—knew that this wasn't a bad dream after all, that Paul was really gone from us—and my heart began to pound, my body wouldn't move; I could feel my heart begin to beat faster and the sweat was making my body clammy. Before I even got out of the car the tears started.

As information was being digested the tears continued and every time I would pull myself together I would look at David, Paul's eight-year-old son, my grandson, and see my beloved Paul Ray standing in front of me. I kept saying, "This can't be true, not my baby," and my heart was beating and all the time my mind knew the truth and the tears wouldn't stop. All day long friends would come and go and I would have to hear the story retold and the tears would come again.

My granddaughter, Jessica, seemed lost in her own thoughts but was somehow going through the motions of holding in her feelings; only a few times did I think she was going to break down. David was off to his friend's house to escape the deep sense of sorrow that permeated the house.

19

I could see the strain and worry in his eyes, those same eyes as his Daddy, soft-brown shadows under them telling me how much he hurt even though he wouldn't shed a tear. As I watched him run off down the street I thought that was the best thing for him; to be with his friends. Birgit tried to be strong and do what was needed of her but naturally these spurts of hostessing were interrupted while she had to excuse herself to talk to friends coming and going; another round of crying.

I watched, trying to stay out of the way. I cried silently, wanting to put on a brave face. I lingered long over my feelings, wishing the mental slideshow that had accompanied me to the base was still running in my head, instead of this more sobering reality.

It was then that I started to write down my feelings, my thoughts, hoping to share them with my son:

April 5, 2003

Thank God for Bradley and Lisa; they seemed to be the only two who know what needs to be done. Bradley took Birgit to the base this morning to start the mountain of paperwork.

Birgit's friends and military wives, who are like her family, keep coming over, bringing food, sitting for a while with faces so ashen white, so scared, knowing that it could have been their loved one.

I see all the activity and seem to be walking in a fog. I watch as if I am not a part of it all but as if I am an observer; to say that this is all so surreal is an under-statement. I feel so hopeless, so utterly helpless and useless. How can I comfort when there is none for myself? I still can't believe what they are saying; my boy would never step off the plane and in my head I refuse to see him coming home any other way.

My head knows the truth but my heart keeps saying it isn't so…

Mid-afternoon

David showed up in the cul-de-sac with a large American flag on a stick; the father of his friend had given it to him. As I watched him, he started to walk around the circle, his little golden head slightly bowed as if in deep medita-tion—or prayer. At one point he changed his step into a slow but steady march; I noticed he was singing ever so softly, as if to himself. As he came in front of the drive I could hear him. He was singing, "I'm proud to be an American…"

The recognition floored me; it was instant, immediate, and evocative. That was always one of your favorite songs, Paul. He looked so much like you at that age that I could no longer hold back the tears. I wanted to run to him and hold him and never let him go. I didn't want to scare him; I knew if I went to him he would surely feel my own fear.

Jessica was so beautiful and still trying not to show her emotions. She seemed to be in a total fog that day, much like myself. A teenager, what was she thinking? She was trying to be so strong for her Mom. I saw very few tears and, instead, saw a girl who was always doing what was needed to be done, going through the motions like the rest of us. She would gladly run to the store for any little thing, trying so hard to be invisible.

You would have been so proud of her, son…

As I watched Birgit, she was trying to get the paperwork done with so much difficulty, sporadic bursts of tears and then a calming; Bradley sat so patiently, thank God for this gentle man.

We have no idea when you will be brought home, Paul, but arrangements will have to be made. Birgit is unable to do this and I am grateful for something to do, no matter how hard this will be…

Tomorrow Lisa and I will do what needs to be done.

April 6, 2003

Lisa and I set out early to look for a place to have your funeral. Words came slow and hard today, both of us dealing with our own thoughts and emotions, trying to be strong for each other…

Pulling up to what appeared an old, white southern mansion, I could hardly believe I was approaching a funeral home for my beloved son. It had large white pillars, wide long porches with big white rocking chairs on them, very old oak trees surrounding the grounds, and a host of azaleas in full bloom in soft pink and white colors. I got an easy feeling as soon as we pulled into the drive. As we walked up the steps to the front door neither of us had anything to say. As we walked into the house my emotions were overwhelming.

Tom Carter, the funeral director, was out back digging in his garden so we went out to meet him. I don't remember much about that day but I do remember that he kept apologizing for not being "clean" and in what he called his "work clothes"; he seemed uneasy as he was explaining that he had critters eating at his vegetables.

He had a smudge of dirt on his face and neither of us mentioned it. When I studied the smudge of dirt on his right check it made me feel like this was an ordinary man and not a mortician. Meeting Tom Carter and talking to him, I think that Lisa and I may have been thinking the same thing: This is a man you would have liked had you ever met him, Paul. He had a gentle and easy way about himself, so much like you...

He made me feel comfortable in his presence and that, in turn, made our job so much easier. As we walked around this old home and then back to his office to talk business I was at last suffused with the feeling of comfort and caring. I think that Lisa and I knew right away that this would be where we would have your funeral. The feeling I got was unpretentious and welcoming.

I don't know how a funeral home could be a welcome place, but I got a warm, fuzzy feeling from this old house as I looked around. I thought about how you would have loved this old home with its high ceilings and fireplace, the huge kitchen; I could almost see you in there cooking.

Arrangements were at last made and now we waited for you to come home. I feel so helpless in my role to console your young family; my grief is like a heavy coat that I am wearing and can't take off. I still keep asking how this could be true, yet here we all are, crying and wishing it wasn't true after all.

It is time for me to go back to Florida. I have worried about Dad so much while I was here and Dad is so sick. I don't even know if he will be able to make it back to Georgia for the funeral.

I know I need to leave but I hate to leave your family

I feel like I am letting them down.

Worse yet, I feel like I am letting *you* down...

3

You're Home

✦

April 12, 2003

You have arrived home in a box with an American flag draped over it and tomorrow we will say good-bye to you. That is how it's done in this man's Army; that is how a soldier finds his final resting place.

When you enlisted it was like we all signed up; I never signed up for this…

Your last e-mail to Dad and I runs through my brain like poison darts hitting my heart. Did you know more than I? Why didn't I listen when you said:

Dear Mom and Dad,

This is the letter no parent wants to get. So I will start by saying this. If it is my time to go, I want you to know this: Parents sacrifice so much to make the lives of their kids better than the one they had and kids often never realize it until they are adults. I think that is why I still haven't thanked you for all you have done. As I sit here getting ready to head into war once again I realize that I have left some things unsaid. I love you and don't want you to worry, even though I know you will until the day I am home again…

At that very moment in time I remembered the last time we said good-bye. "Mom," you told me, "don't worry about me. I'll be fine, just take care of Dad and I will see you soon."

I believed you because you had left before and come home so many other times. There was something different this time; I felt that this good-bye was so tense. The look on your face told me you were worried and I thought it was about Dad so I didn't pay much attention.

I'm sure now that was part of it, but there was something…different…in your eyes that day. Your hug was a little longer and tighter, as if perhaps you knew it could be the last one we'd ever share. How could a son know more than his mother?!? I never considered it would be the last time I would see you alive. Later, when talking to friends and family, they too said that there was a difference in the way you said good-bye but no one could put a finger on it.

As I recall your final e-mail it all suddenly seems so clear:

There are two ways to come home, stepping off the plane and being carried off the plane. It doesn't matter how I come home because I am prepared to give all that I am to insure that all my boys make it home. It is my privilege to be given twenty-five of the finest Americans we call soldiers to lead into war. Many are young and don't understand what they are about to face, just that they are away from the ones they love…

The letter was never signed and I often wonder if there was more you wanted to say—maybe you left it unfinished because you always thought you'd get back to it—or perhaps you were just too worried to say any more. I had never received a letter like this from you when you were in other wars and, again, I wonder if you knew that your destiny was close at hand.

Sadly, now I will never know if there was more you needed to say…

I know there is much more I have to say, though. I'll try doing it here, now, in these words to you. Can you hear them? Now, when you need your mother most of all, all I can do is share my thoughts, my feelings, my hopes, my pain.

I'll start with the latest: News from the front lines of battle says you are a hero; you saved many lives. Why didn't God save you? Yes, you saved your boys but what about us, the family you left behind? What do we do now?

How do we go on without you?

Who will save *us*?

4

The Funeral

Today, as we prepare to say goodbye to you, there is hardly a breeze to speak of; the sun is high and it is very hot. It is almost as if the wind knows not to interfere; as if Mother Nature herself is paying her respects by bowing out and leaving us all to our own devices.

We arrived all in black: family, friends, brothers in arms, commanders and chiefs. It is time. As Dad and I walked into the funeral home Tom Carter was there to greet us in his Sunday best; I almost didn't recognize him out of his overalls.

I could smell the potent air filled with flowers, the sickly sweet scent already testing my fragile stomach, making me wonder if I could really do this after all. As Tom escorted us to the chapel my eyes first met the rich wood of your teak coffin and I could hardly walk.

My steps faltered and I couldn't breathe. There was no air left in the room. Entering into the chapel proper I saw Bradley supporting my Lisa, who had collapsed onto the floor next to your casket, crying uncontrollably in Bradley's arms with him trying to soothe her with soft words.

My heart was breaking for her; she was so close to you and loved you so much. She has been trying to be strong for everyone else, how will she go on without you? Who will be strong for her when the strongest man she ever knew is gone?

I see Birgit with her face white as a sheet; she is standing there staring at you like she was looking at a stranger, her hands to her mouth as if to stifle a scream and Jessica holding her up.

God, I don't want to see my precious son like this. As I slowly walked to your casket I kept hoping that when I looked in, you would not be there and someone else would be, then I would know that the Army had made a terrible mistake. The name Smith was so common and I would wake up and this would have all been a very long—a very bad—dream.

I had to make sure that it is really you, Paul. I guess confirming for the last time that it really is you. As I walked toward the coffin past the red, white and blue flowers that had my nose stinging with the smell of death my steps faltered again but this time Dad was there to hold me up.

As I stood there looking into this box with your body in it, I knew this was something I had to do. As I looked at the face that appeared to be asleep, I knew at once it was you. There was no need to pinch myself; this was no nightmare. It was real; this was true, and final.

Silently, gravely I marveled at the perfection of your dress uniform but was not surprised; I noted that all your medals were shining so bright, and knew nothing less would have been right.

As I touched your heart to say a prayer I could feel my own breaking in two; it felt as if there was a hand inside of me trying to tear my heart out, it hurt so bad I just wanted to die right there. I'd heard people say that before but I never knew what it felt like to want to die—literally, just stop living right at that very moment—until I saw your peaceful form lying in state.

Looking at your face I thought that it was a wax figure of you that I was looking at. It was you…but not you. Your eyes didn't seem to be the same shape that they always were; they seemed flat. Your eyelashes were too small. I remember how long they were when you were trying to flirt with me and barter for something. Your head looked as if it was more in the shape of a platter rather then oval shaped. Such strange thoughts for a mother at her son's funeral, and yet these were the emotions, these were the feelings that came rushing to my head.

I could no more control them than I could the fact that you were gone…

My medical background informed me; I knew why you looked the way you did, but didn't want to think of how the bullet must have torn out the back of your whole head, resulting in the different shape. Looking at you, I just thanked God that this person didn't really resemble my beautiful son. Now my memories of you would always have your face, your eyes, your happy smile.

As I stood there with my hand on your heart I felt the cigar in the pocket of your coat beneath the medal and assumed that it was your victory cigar. The word "victory" stuck in my mind and I became so angry I wanted to scream; my eyes stung with tears filled with so much hate. Hate for who—and what—I wasn't sure.

All I could think of was: What victory? Victory for whom? It certainly wasn't a victory for me. I was laying my son to rest today, and I would never again see him in the world; there would never be victory for me ever again.

Your father's gentle hand interrupted my vengeful reverie. Dad led me to our seats and the service started. As music swelled I let my tearful eyes wander around the room. The flowers were many and mostly in red, white and blue. The chapel was packed and hot. The air was charged with an electricity I couldn't explain; it was as if all our hopes, dreams, disappointment, and grief held some kind of magnetic charge, pulling us closer together even as it tore us all apart.

I was so surprised at all the people that had come to say goodbye to you. Old friends from school; I had long forgotten their names. Old neighbors and acquaintances, co-workers and peers. So many military men from the various clubs in town; they were there to honor my hero and pay their respects to the family. Only later would I realize how far they had all driven to share one last moment with you. Your beloved friend, Greg, and his lovely wife, Heather, were there. He was always there for you, Paul. I couldn't imagine him not being here today.

I felt that the air was hanging heavy over us and would soon suffocate all in attendance. The service was befitting of a hero, but despite the heaping of praise and stoic testimonials I wasn't able to concentrate on what was being said. My mind was filled with so much anger; my heart with so much pain that I just wanted to be anyplace but here; I still wanted to die.

As your coffin passed and we started to walk out, Birgit stood and slowly sank to the floor; her eyes had rolled back in her head and then she passed out. There were so many people gathering around her to help, I knew that I could do nothing so Dad and I walked out to the canopy that was set up outside under the grandfather oaks that provided some relief from the merciless sun.

Soon the rest of the family joined us under the bright blue canopy that suddenly made me wish we hadn't ordered it; I felt like I was closed in. The air was oppressive and still. Your beautiful teak coffin draped with our red, white and blue was set outside in the driveway and the hearse parked not far off.

Suddenly Birgit and the rest of the family were seated and waiting. The crisis had passed; the show must go on. The service was like that; events came in fast forward and rewind, pause and freeze frame. For instance, I only barley remember hearing the bag pipes playing "Amazing Grace" in the background, the song that you wanted in the event that we all were here for, this final farewell.

Next, the twenty-one gun salute that shook the very core of everyone's soul seemed to come out of nowhere. I know it's tradition, but the jarring sound of all those rifle reports only made the reality of your death so much clearer. Were those the final sounds that met your ear? The shuddering tear of bullets piercing the air? What a horrible, tragic, ghastly farewell.

The flag that draped your coffin was folded with so much love and care that the process seemed to move in slow motion; I was mesmerized by the act of it all, lulled into a surreal state where I was not a participant but an observer. Then I heard "Taps" being played and the mournful goodbye signaled the loss of control for all who loved you so. Now my mind was so numb and the unwanted tears would not abate.

What I didn't hear or remember was what was said to me before the American flag was put in my hands, something about "America" and "the president." Perhaps I heard but, out of anger or despair, blocked out the words and their meaning.

Soon your casket was being put into the back of the hearse; it was at that moment that Birgit completely fell apart, she had done well up to this point. She ran to the hearse and hugged the casket, knowing that it was her last chance to touch you even though I knew you were not in there, but home with our Lord. I knew that I would never be the same person I once was, I knew I would never smile or be happy ever again.

Was it age that made our reaction so different? Or the subtle difference between a mother's love and that of her son's spouse? Perhaps, in the end, we all choose to grieve differently. No, that's not quite right either; there is no choice but to grieve completely, totally and absolutely.

We don't control our grief; it controls us...

The contribution you made to this country and the people that thank you for your sacrifice were far more then I had ever expected it to be. As Birgit faced her own personal demons I reflected on the gamble we'd all taken the day we let you go to basic training. We all knew that this end was a possibility but no one wanted to think about it or, now, believe that it had come to its fruition.

The "what ifs" had finally come home to roost...

In Memory of

SFC PAUL RAY SMITH

Born
El Paso, Texas
Sept. 24, 1969
Died
Baghdad, Iraq
April 4, 2003

Services
Chapel
Saturday, April 12, 2003
11:00 A.M.
Ministers

Roger Wilkins

Paul Was A Proud American
Dedicated Husband and Father

Taps
Day is done, gone the sun
from the lake, from the hill,
from the sky.
All is well, safely rest. God is nigh.

Thanks and praise for our days
'neath the sun, 'neath the stars,
'neath the sky.
As we go, this we know. God is nigh.

Thomas L. Carter Funeral Home
1822 East Oglethorpe Hwy
Hinesville, GA 31313
912-876-5095

In Memory

5

Remembering You

✦

April 15, 2003

My heart is so heavy today. My sadness so deep as I sit on the patio, yet I can't help but smile as my memories take me back to last spring when you and the kids and all your siblings, nieces and nephews were here to celebrate Easter. The joy that our Lord had risen was only celebrated more ecstatically because my family was here having so much fun. I could hear the laughter that flowed in and out of the house, a sound I longed for still.

Last year our family circle had been complete. (What a difference a year could make; now no Easter would ever be the same.) In my mind's eye I could see you in the backyard, tall, being silly with all the kids, looking so tired but never too tired to help Greyson and Jared look for Easter eggs.

Later in the day I saw you playing in the pool with all the kids. I had to laugh at you because you were acting as much a kid as the kids were. They all loved playing with you because you never got mad at them when they would jump on you or splash you or hit you with balls, instead you just gave it right back to them. Like a kid would do. What a gift to share; that childhood innocence in such a fine adult.

Did you know the gifts you had? Did you know how much we loved you? How much the children loved you? They all wanted to play with Uncle Paul and be tossed around like a rag doll in the pool.

Who wouldn't?

Later, cooking on the grill like a master chef while Dad stood watch over you to make sure you did it right, although even when you did something your own way—and not how you'd been taught—he never did say a word.

I can't help but remember that no matter what you did, you always put your all into it; building something, fixing something, always taking the time to explain yourself and what you were doing to whoever was with you.

I remember how you yelled at the kids for running by the deep end of the pool, even while you cautioned others to stay clear of the hot grill. I swear, sometimes you reminded me of a Mother hen looking after her chicks; you were such a good Dad. Now that is all I have, the memories of you.

What a bittersweet joy; to have the memories but not the man who made them. God, please let it be enough. I just can't stand this new life I am living without you.

9:00 p.m.
Same Day

I went out to look at the moon this evening, but it wasn't up yet. The North Star was very bright, but when I looked to the south, I hoped that the bright pulsing star I was looking at was you and that you knew all I was feeling in my heart.

As I sat alone and tried to see your face among the stars I couldn't help but remember the talk you had with David before you left for the war. I can see you sitting in the swing outside your house in Georgia; your arms around David telling him that if you didn't return all he would have to do is look up at that pulsing star and he would know you were there with him.

As I looked up into the night sky I swear I heard you say, "It's okay Mom, I'm fine and I do know what you are feeling." I could feel the love and tenderness you must have felt with him. I pray that David never forgets the little things that he had with you; the tender moments between father and son. I know how much love you put into those little things with him.

This much I promise you, Paul: I won't let him forget...

6

Another Good-bye

♦

April 17, 2003

A TRAVELER COMING HOME

A traveler ventured forth one day
Upon a long and winding road
With faith and trust to lead the way
With strength and will to bear his load.
And at a slow but steady pace,
In cold of storm, in warmth of sun.
He journeyed on from place to place
And gained some value from each one.
Until at last one quiet night,
He climbed a hill's soft-rounding crest
And saw afar a single light
That seemed to promise peace and rest,
And following its glow, He came
Upon the house in which it shone.
A voice inside called out his name
And told him he was truly home.
Now all of us
Must travel too---
Like his, our paths wind slowly on,
And surely when
The course is through
A welcome comfort waits beyond
May we believe that sweet content
Is earned by all those miles passed
And never doubt
Each traveler's meant
To reach a loving home at last.

Will it ever end? I said good-bye to you again today, only this time it felt real and permanent. Another funeral here in Florida for your friends that weren't able to make the one in Georgia, as well as the many veteran friends of the family that wanted to pay you honor and respect.

Once again we all entered in black, so many people that knew you and those that only knew us, and they signed the guest book and waited to pay their respects. Today the difference is that in place of a sleek, shiny, teakwood coffin there is a silver and brass urn that holds your ashes and an oversized picture of you that stands on a tripod.

It was another passing; another distancing of you from me. More of you was gone this time, but the pain was just as intense. I find myself in a time warp of grief, a loop that never ends guiding my life from one endless, tearful hour to the next. I can only imagine what Birgit and the children are going through.

Once again the flowers made me sick to my stomach; there are so many and again they are all red, white and blue. The funeral home is packed—standing room only—and I don't even know who they all are. God, will this ever end? I feel like this is going on forever. Will I ever have closure? Will I ever find peace?

Bradley gave your eulogy; he said "you were the right man at the right time." He also said, "At your sister Lisa's wedding, when she became so nervous about last minute details you took over and took care of every thing in a quiet unassuming way."

He told the story of the fishing expedition with your family. With waves cresting six feet, how while he was eating Dramamine you fixed the stalled engine 22 miles out to sea with only a pair of pliers and a knife that was used to prep the fish, saving your whole family that day.

He repeated what he had said earlier, how you were "The right man at the right time." He went on to say that you were a family man, you loved your wife and kids, you were a friend. He talked about how you made him feel comfortable from the very beginning, and how you shared great stories.

He talked about your "quiet grace" in how you lived your life and did what "had to be done." He said you could always be counted on and your soldiers and country did just that; counted on you. You were "the right man at the right time...at the wrong place." He wanted to share with everyone there the most important thing you taught him. Not by words, but by deed: "Live here in the now and cherish your family, your friends, and your country."

After the service our church had set up a buffet lunch served at the home that was once your refuge, and which now belongs to your family. There was so much food and so many people; how you would have loved to talk to them all. Why don't we have funerals before they're necessary?

Dad and I had a bite to eat and then excused ourselves and went home to rest before the sun set. Just thinking about what was to come had me so tired that I just needed to be quiet and rest a bit. I just needed some time; a little time to be alone and still. There was still more time to grieve, and more people to share our grief with. We knew that most guests would go home and this would leave only close friends that were invited to the docks with the family.

There was still one last voyage for you to take…

5:00 P.M.

As we all meet back at Birgit's house I can see the exhaustion on the faces of my family and I am so glad that Dad and I went home when we did, not that we were any more rested then we were before.

We all know that this is truly the last good-bye and I can see that we are all ready for it to be over. We load into cars that will take us to the docks in New Port Richey to board the Miss Virginia fishing boat; no better a vessel to take you to your final resting place.

The drive is quiet and I feel too tired to even cry anymore. I am sure there are no more tears left anyway. I know that this is the final road that we will travel together, Paul, and the last time I will say good-bye to you.

At last, I am ready.

The captain is waiting for us, greeting us and giving condolences. *How many families has he taken out to sea for this very purpose?* I wonder. He seems prepared, anyway, and has stocked the boat with snacks for the kids and drinks for the adults. It's another act of selfless service; he was never asked to do any of this. In fact, it was his gift to the family, as was the ride. All of this because he simply wanted to thank us for your service to your country. It is at times like these that I still believe our country is worth fighting for. I only wish I felt that way more often.

As I sit inside the enclosed area of the boat at a booth, one like you would find in any diner, I look out over the water that's churning in our wake and I think of the many times that you and Dad must have seen this very same view.

There is little time for reflection and even less for tears; my children are all wandering inside and then out, looking so lost in a sea of activity and so sad without you, their moral, physical, and paternal compass. All of them inside their own heads with so much pain on their faces.

Tony sits holding Devon on his lap, both of them looking so lost. I see such pain in his eyes; I know he will be glad when today is over and he can return to his inward self. He hates for people to see behind his eyes and witness his pain.

Lisa and Bradley are standing at the railing talking softly to each other; my Lisa's eyes are so swollen and red from crying. What are they saying to each other? What words can pass between two who feel so much grief? I know it will take her a long time to be normal again, if ever. Will any of us ever be normal again?

What *is* normal, anyway?

The boat is slowing now and has maneuvered around so that the back of the boat faces the sunset; then the engines stop. The sudden quiet is startling; again it's like Mother Nature has afforded you another window of opportunity, another moment of earthly silence. The sun is just starting to touch the horizon and Birgit turns on the portable tape player she brought with her.

We all gather at the back of the boat. Earlier, Birgit had asked me if I would put your urn in the water and I said I would. Now Birgit is playing your song together, "You're still the one." And as the sun begins to sink low she sings a love song to you for the last time. She cries and holds your urn close to her heart; it is almost more than I can take and as she hands me your urn with your ashes, it becomes a moment frozen in time.

I can't move or breathe. I don't want to let you go, somehow I thought that if I just stood still at the railing of this boat and held your urn I would be able to go on, and you would somehow be home again.

As your ashes fall I know this not to be true...

Do not stand at my grave and weep,
I am not there, I do not sleep.
I am a thousand winds that blow,
I am the diamond glints on snow.

I am the sunlight on ripened grain,
I am the autumn's gentle rain.
When you waken in the morning's hush,
I am the swift uplifting rush
Of quiet birds in circled flight.
I am the soft stars that shine at night.

Do not stand at my grave and cry,
I am not there, I did not die.

Thomas B. Dobies Funeral Home
New Port Richey, Florida

IN MEMORY OF

SFC Paul Ray Smith

BORN
September 24, 1969
El Paso, Texas

DIED
April 4, 2003
in Iraq

TIME AND PLACE OF SERVICE
Thursday, April 17, 2003
Eleven O'Clock AM
Thomas B. Dobies Funeral Home
6616 Congress Street
New Port Richey, Florida

OFFICIATING
Pastor Mike Hughes
Pastor Tom Buck

MUSICIAN
Bagpiper from the
Amvets Post #98

Later That Same Evening...

I laid you to rest today in the warm waters off Anclote Key, where you and Dad often went to fish. As the sky turned pink with streaks of orange, the sun was setting, the wind was still, the reflection of the sun on the water was picture perfect.

I knew it was a sunset you would have stood and watched until it was gone.

Dad said something to me and I realized that I was just standing still and not breathing. As I gently let your urn slip through my hands I thought that I would surely die. I watched the urn sink slowly, then I released two dozen white butterflies while your friends and family placed flowers in the water off the Miss Virginia fishing boat. What a sad, stunning, beautiful affair it was.

In the darkening sky the butterflies fluttered into the sunset, looking ethereal and translucent; 24 angels bound for heaven. All the flowers in the water made me think of a Chinese funeral. It looked so peaceful and then the sun sank below the horizon and was gone.

I said good-bye to you for the last time.

Rest well, my son, in the warm waters of your beloved Florida; we will miss you so much. The ride back to the docks was solemn and sad. When we got back the family hugged and kissed, our friends said they were sorry for our loss, and then we all went our separate ways. We all went home to mourn in our own way. I never wanted to get out of bed again.

I did so only to write these words.

Please tell me you can hear them...

7

July 4, 2003

Independence Day. How strange the words sound on my tongue. With the loss of you, today is a day that will never again be a celebration full of hot dogs and fireworks, Kool-Aid and watermelon. Oh, how you loved the fireworks.

As a teenager you never would listen to me when I said you couldn't buy any. No matter how much I protested or threatened, you always did, and I always acted like I didn't know. At the time I had no idea why you were so fascinated with things that popped and blew up. All boys love fireworks; it's a right of passage, or so I suppose. But you seemed obsessed with them in a way that went beyond the norm.

The look in your eyes as they sizzled and popped, soared into the night sky, screaming the whole way before their shattering explosion; I'll never forget it. Thinking back, I can't believe that you and Greg never blew up the garage, the house or even yourselves.

Today I know all too well why you loved them so much; it was to be part of your destiny.

Although we will pass the day in somber reflection it is still a celebration of sorts, for today the whole nation thanks you—and honors you—for the freedom that you and all fallen heroes have given to us. In spite of all the honors to which you are so rightfully entitled in so many ways my joy is overpowered by my extreme sadness.

Your whole family was invited to the AMVETS club today to celebrate the 4th of July holiday, but I don't feel like celebrating or even getting out of bed, for that matter. Still, if it's in your honor I can hardly resist. Any excuse to be closer to where you are, to be near you for one second, even if it's in name only.

So I went. The club that you and Dad would go to just to get away from "us girls" for a spell was decorated with flags, and everywhere you looked you could see red, white and blue. It reminded me of the flowers at your funeral. One wall of the club was adorned with your picture and a book that tells your story.

How proud I was to see it all, just for you.

When we got to the club we learned that we were to be the guests of honor and, of course, the media was there. I was not up for the spotlight today; I just wanted to crawl into a hole at the very least. Lisa and the kids were here from Atlanta. As the kids ran around in the dining room I could see they were getting over heated but it didn't seem to bother them.

Tony's children were also showing signs of the heat. In fact, we were all very hot and, no wonder: the temperature was in the nineties. As the day wore down and I grew tired of smiling and saying thanks to all who gave condolences, I could see in the eyes of my children and grandchildren that they, too, had had enough and knew that they would have much rather been at your house playing in the pool, celebrating and paying their respects the same way they celebrated you in life. The club is naming the dinning room after you; they have honored you with pictures and posters on the wall and want as much as we can give them to add to the memorabilia that they already have.

I soon learned there was work to do before we got home to that pool or even our own thoughts. The interviews all started with the same questions, and ones that we had already answered a hundred times by now. I could hardly blame the press for their interest but I wondered sometimes whether they saw beyond the camera lens to the person they were interviewing. Couldn't they tell how tired we were? How sad and lonely and missing you we were?!?

I sometimes wondered if it would mater if they did…

As the last interview was winding down one of the reporters asked how we felt about you being nominated for the Medal-of-Honor. We all just sat there as if we didn't want to answer and then your brother, Tony, with much pain in his eyes, said simply, "We would rather have him home." How poignantly those six simple words expressed the sentiments of your whole family.

After that the day continued to turn hotter and sticky; the kids were getting fussy and one by one we began to leave. The day was nice but maybe too soon for me to be talking to the press.

On the way home Dad informed me that at a certain point in the day I had just shut down; he said that he tried to tell me but I seemed to be so far away that I really didn't hear him. I don't remember that moment but certainly wasn't surprised that I had—and sure wasn't going to start apologizing for myself now. I don't know what people want from me. How can I act normal when my life has been turned upside down?

I'm sorry, but today I really don't give a damn what anyone thinks.

We didn't see the fireworks tonight, the first time I can remember that we didn't.

Were there fireworks where you are, Paul?

Desert Storm
1991

I remembered when you got home from Desert Storm, how changed you were. I remembered the look in your eyes that said so much and yet never spoke a word. The few details that you did talk to us about made me believe the horrors of the war that you only wanted to forget. As a mother who'd had her share of nightmares, I knew they would haunt your dreams for many years to come.

Even the way you talked had changed. The things that you did say mostly were sentences like "…if I had only," or, "maybe if I would have only done," or, "if I would have been in that place." Sentences not finished but with so much doubt, and even guilt, I could still see haunting your eyes.

At that time I thought back to when I was a child and my mother's brother, my Uncle Bill, would tell us terrible stores of World War II when he was a prisoner of war. Just like you, he also wore those same eyes. As a civilian I will never know or understand the horror of war and I can't even imagine what your beautiful eyes had seen.

I only wished I could make them smile once more…

Your Welcome Home Party

You rode your motorcycle into the backyard of our new house on the river for your welcome home party looking like a kid once more; your eyes were the only thing that looked old about you. That was one of the happiest days of my life; as long as I live I will never forget it.

That morning I couldn't put enough yellow ribbons or yellow balloons on the trees lining the street and the long driveway that led to the house. Talk about following the yellow brick road! I tried my hardest to show my appreciation of all you'd done; how well you'd served your country. I was so proud. The "Welcome Home Hero" signs were everywhere they could stick and the one very large banner stretched between the two large oak trees in the backyard.

As the family and friends waited for your arrival we all said silent prayers, thanking God for bringing you home safely; we were all so proud of you. Lisa and Cris waited in the kitchen where the cake was sitting on the table waiting for you. (Yes, of course, your favorite.)

I saw icing missing from the side and knew that one of them had to have a taste, but I knew you wouldn't care. More of your friends were arriving and the smell of charcoal was thick in the air. Dad and his friend Chuck were the chefs for the day; I think they thought you were bringing the whole army home with you, for the amount of food cooking was beyond a lot, and much to my surprise there really wasn't a lot leftover when all was said and done. I was so anxious for you to arrive, I kept going to the door and peeking out the front windows while the girls kept telling me I was "wearing out the floor" and then laughing at me.

As if some big Hollywood mogul was directing the scene you arrived at just the right time: I was standing by the grill and had a perfect view of the yard were you pulled in between the trees. I still couldn't believe that you were really there. The look on your face told me how happy you were with all the fuss we made, even though you would never say anything beyond a quick and stilted, "Thanks, mom."

But a mother knows; I saw it all in your eyes...

Going into the house for the first time you spotted your old teddy bear, which I had placed on one of the chairs in a corner of the living room. It leaned against your grandfather's American flag, which was once the cover for his casket. I had put them there when you left for the war and before I knew it you were taking the flag and, with Dad's help, I watched as the two of you hoisted it up the flag-pole near the water's edge.

I couldn't help but count my many blessings as the flag tousled in the thin summer breeze, as if protecting us all from harm: my whole family was gathered together with friends of all ages and once more I felt that the family was complete.

The day was turning out perfectly, the sun warm but a gentle breeze off the water making for a most pleasant feel in the yard. Under the giant trees with the limbs stretched out to provide shade we all stayed cool. We watched the fiercely competitive volley ball game that you and friends were having in the vacant field that Dad had cut the day before so the net could be stretched away from the tables and chairs. The cutthroat game was worthy of ESPN but you and your friends could have cared less; it didn't matter who was watching, you brought your best and played to win, no matter what the game or who the opponent.

Throughout the day I loved watching all my kids and grandchildren playing games, being silly, and just letting their hair down and having fun. I thought to myself often that day, "...this is the day the Lord has made. This is what family is all about."

As I watched you play with your nieces, giving them all rides on your motor-cycle or tossing horse shoes with them, I couldn't help but think how lucky they were to have an uncle like you; one who cared so much for them and gave of him-self so that they could enjoy the day as much as you were. I watched as the games continued. Then came the inevitable rides down the river with a great deal of fishing off the dock.

As I sit here writing this I can see that day as if it were all going on at this very minute, yet it was so long ago; a different boy in a different world on a different day in a different lifetime. That was a wonderful celebration of you and your return home, and a darn good party to boot. I couldn't believe how much food was cooked and how many beverages had been consumed that day. That was a day to go into the family album, that's for sure.

Christmas, 2001

Dad and I rented three cabins in the Georgia Mountains for one week and for once we were all there to celebrate the holidays. Other than your welcome home party from Desert Storm, that was the very last time the whole family was ever all together again.

I was so excited; I wanted this to be a real, old-fashioned Christmas. Every mother has the same dream, I suppose, but to be able to make it a reality was a blessing in disguise, especially looking back in retrospect.

I know that Dad thought I was totally out of my mind, and that I should just wait till we got to the mountains to buy the things that I insisted we pack instead. Whether it was just the Christmas spirit or true insanity I will never know, but one can forgive a mother for going overboard when her holiday wishes finally come true!

I must have packed at least three dozen cookie cutters. Whatever the number, I know that it was every one I owned and—though I never told your father—a few that I bought special for the occasion. Some were for baking cookies with the grand kids and others for making ornaments for the three live trees I planned to buy there in Georgia; one for each cabin.

Then there was an assortment of colored construction paper to make paper chains for the trees, as well as tons of different colored glitter and anything else I thought I might need. I brought enough decorations for five cabins, but you can never have enough lights and wreaths as far as I was concerned.

Each cabin had a fireplace that was as tall as the second floor bedrooms. One of the bedrooms had an open window that looked down over the living room and had a great view of the kitchen; there was also a fireplace and a deck that had a panoramic view of the mountains.

Each cabin had a hot tub off the master bedroom downstairs that had sliding doors on both the bedroom and the living room. (The kids sure got a kick out of that!) The hot tub room also had a deck with the same beautiful view as the living room. My Christmas pictures from that year deserved their very own album and already we were making plans to do this again.

Sadly, it was never meant to be...

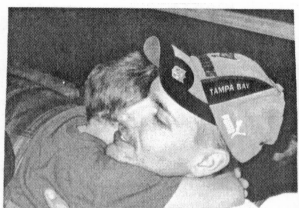

August, 2003
Paul's Boys

Your boys are back from Iraq and I am going to see them. You, Paul, are the reason I feel so compelled to welcome your boys home. It was the things you said—and the things that you didn't say—after Desert Storm. Birgit and I drove to Fort Stewart together, where we met up with Lisa.

The next day we went to your company and were escorted out to the back parking lot where your boys were in formation waiting for us. The August sun was baking and the perspiration was very noticeable on the men standing at attention. As Birgit first addressed the men and then your sister talked to them, I don't know what they said because I stood and I looked into the faces of so many boys and young men. The hot, sweaty faces overrode what was being said in my ears. As I scanned each face I saw your sweet face, your eyes, I saw your tears and felt the pain you must have felt knowing the truth. That maybe some of these boys would not make it back home.

Little did we know…

Looking out over the scene in front of me I knew why. I knew why you gave up time fishing with David and riding your motorcycle with Jessica. It was for these boys that you cared so much about. I remember you telling me, "…if I would have only done this or that, things would have turned out differently."

I always felt that somehow you blamed yourself for things that happened out there in the desert. Today, as I look out at your boys I want to make sure that they knew first how much you cared for them and second that there was nothing they either did or did not do that would have changed the course of that day.

You did everything you could have possibly done to teach them what they needed to know to keep them as safe as possible in battle. You trained them harder and longer only because you *did* care about them and, in the end, you *did* save your boys. There were not many others lost because of what you did teach them. You had reached the end of your destiny and it was God's will that called you home.

As I stood in the sultry heat and spoke to the men that stood in formation before me, I saw heartfelt tears and I prayed:

"God, please let me make a difference, let me praise them for the job they did well and let me say just one something that would somehow ease the pain I saw in so many pairs of eyes. Let them know that there was nothing they could have done on that terrible day other than what they did do…"

Then I just wanted to hug every man that stood before me and tell them that I was so glad they were home. We met with Captain Smith that day. He asked if our lives were "getting back to normal." I understood the question but I couldn't help but think to myself: Normal, how could things ever be normal again?

We then visited Warriors Walk. Fort Stewart had planted two rows of red bud trees, one on each side of a sidewalk that is adjacent to the parade field. Each tree planted was to be in memory of a soldier that fell in the sands of Iraq. As we approached the walkway, I saw the line of red buds and my heart sank because I knew I would find your marker among them. Your tree seemed taller than the others, stronger too, and perhaps that was just an illusion because that is how I always viewed you.

Lisa was still wearing her mask to hide her pain. I saw behind her mask today as she knelt and touched your name on the marker that sits in front of your tree. She is so beautiful and so sad. I wish I could make the pain in her go away, but again, in her own time. She touched your nameplate so tenderly that it broke my heart. She held her pain and tears in; she is very brave, just like you Paul, unlike me who wears her emotions on the outside for all to see.

August 23, 2003

We celebrated Jessie's and Olivia Rae's birthday today. Lisa came down from Atlanta. Tony and his family, your friend Greg and his lovely wife and kids were here, too. Everyone was here but your little sister, Crissy.

As I watched Greg I knew that your plans were to retire here in Florida. I tried to visualize you and your family with Greg and his family. How you would have loved hanging out together, smiling with pride at your assembled families and "out bragging" each other with your children's accomplishments, but somehow the pictures never came to me; this only added to my pain.

I missed you so much today, with your silliness and your pranks. I missed the laughter that was always a part of you and so much a part of this house, which now houses Birgit, David and Jessie; but I can't hear you today.

At least my eyes are full. When I look at David, I see you. Paul, he has become the song in my heart and I can't ever think of him not being around me. I know he misses you but, like you, he keeps his feelings in the secret place hidden down deep inside. Help guide me, Paul, for I so want to help him in any way I can; I don't want to let you down so I'm counting on you.

The presents were opened; squeals of delight from little Rae and Jessie somewhat quiet. I couldn't help but wonder if she was thinking of her last year's birthday, spent with you. What a difference a year makes, especially to a child. How confusing this must be for them; how sad and terribly lonely.

This morning I looked at last year's birthday pictures, which I have stored on my computer. The roses you bought her along with her sweet sixteen necklace and the cake that was on the table showed the tender heart you had for her. The pretend spanking you were giving her in those pictures, the twinkle in your eyes and the beautiful smile on her face were treasures in our album of treasures. Today she is wearing the sweet sixteen necklace that you gave her last year. Was she seeing those pictures in her mind as I did this morning on the computer?

There was one last present on the patio table and it was for Jessica from Aunt Lisa and Uncle Bradley. It was a small box and when she opened it tears came to her eyes and she held it close to her heart.

"Come on Jess, show us," we all urged in unison.

To our amazement, the little box contained a car key. After your death Lisa and Brad took your Jeep—the one you loved so much and the very one you taught Jessie to change the oil in—all the way up to Atlanta and they had it all fixed up for Jess for her birthday.

Jessica got your Jeep today; she was so happy yet so tearful. This was a rare emotion to see in Jessie, to see her cry like that. I wish I could know her inner feelings and thoughts, to know why she cried, for joy or loss but most likely for both. It's hard to tell with Jess; she, too, thinks she has to be strong for everyone, not to mention the fact that she is a teenager.

The happy day turned bittersweet in more ways than one: Your grandma was put in Hospice this month and it doesn't look very good. We have already lost you and your Uncle Max this year; I don't know if I could take losing my mother, too. Some days I think I will lose my mind over the losses and I can't believe that my plate is big enough for another loss.

Once more I ask myself: Will it ever end?!?

October 2, 2003

When I woke up this morning there was a piece of paper lying where my feet came in contact with the floor. I know it wasn't there last night when I went to bed. How it got there I haven't a clue, maybe it fell out of a book I'm reading or fell out of an old purse I was looking in, I really don't know.

As I bent to pick it up and held it between my fingers I got a tingling feeling wherever paper touched flesh. The paper read: "Paul. Ticket. Delta. 10:00." I knew right away it was when you went to Atlanta to be at your sister Lisa's wedding.

Why was that paper on the floor this morning and, more importantly, where did it come from? Was it a sign from you? Or were you just saying, "Good morning, Mom"?

I stayed in bed a long time today thinking about Lisa's wedding and trying to remember every little detail, especially the ones that I may have missed at the time. I remembered how you flew in from Germany and how tired you look, so preoccupied in your own thoughts.

Finally, you started to relax a little and you became all consumed with the reason you were in Atlanta: Your sister's wedding. When Lisa became nervous with the last minute details you reassured her you would take care of everything, and in your quiet, professional, take charge way, you did just that; you quickly set about making sure everything was perfect so that she wouldn't have to worry about a thing. Not a single detail escaped your intense gaze. Every chair in place, all the flowers fresh, and every candle lit for the sunset service.

Then the wedding started, as Dad walked Lisa down the white runner under all the huge trees that made a canopy for her to walk under. I watched the faces of my loved ones. Lisa so beautiful in her white Cinderella wedding gown, she stared ahead at the man waiting for her under the white arch that was decorated with such care, the light from the candelabras caught in her eyes and I was so happy for her.

A most silly thought ran across my brain but became so real: I told her she would find her frog prince in Atlanta—when she left Florida I even bought her a music box that played, "Someday, My Prince Will Come"—and here we all were at the most beautiful wedding I had ever seen.

Your father walking like a proud peacock, chest stuck out, head held high and when I looked closely, I noted a tear in his eye. I never did ask him what he was thinking of at that precise time, but I'm pretty sure that whatever it was they were tears of joy, happiness, and hope.

Cristina looked so pretty that day and as she watched Lisa become Mrs. Bradley DeVane I thought I saw a whisper of envy in those funny colored eyes of hers that seemed to turn from light brown to almost cat yellow.

I don't get to see your brother, Tony, in a suit very often and I still can't get over what a handsome man he is. Watching you I couldn't help but think how thin and tired looking you were, and sat wondering why—and how I could fix it.

The vows were said as Lisa and Bradley stood under the arch and the light from the candelabras on each side of them seemed to symbolize how a bright new life had begun for them both. At the same time my heart sang; they looked so in love and so happy.

The wedding pictures were taken, and now the reception started on the deck of the grounds and still you were running around madly, making sure everything was perfect for your big sister's wedding. At one point I saw you start to relax a bit but in your eyes there was always a shadow that told me your thoughts were still bothering you. Still, you were not one to let your own troubles stand in the way of another's joy and happiness. I watched as you admired the ongoing festivities, and loved seeing you dance with your sister. When you danced with Cristina I saw the care and concern you had for her.

I had so looked forward to your visit but amidst all the out of town guests and demands for your attention, you and I had such limited time to just sit and talk or visit that day. Too soon after the wedding you were back on a plane on your way back to your boys; you always called them "your boys."

More than anything you left unsaid, that made me realize that you always felt responsible for these men. If we had known then that we would have so little time left, I wonder what we would have said to each other.

As I sat looking around at all my children, I knew I could not have been blessed more; God was so good to me. Each of my children here, healthy, beautiful and helping to celebrate the birth of a new union, Lisa and Bradley's wedding, I am blessed.

If only I could feel the same way today...:

8

The Song in My Heart

✦

October 9, 2003

We took David to Homosassa Springs this weekend to go fishing. As always, we stayed at our favorite campground, Nature's End. We rented one of the trailers that are parked right on the river's edge. David thought it was really neat the way we could open the back door and sit on the small porch and just throw the fishing line right in the river.

Like so many of our outings lately, it was a bittersweet trip. Dad's health still seems to be declining and I worry about him so much. He really didn't feel up to the trip but came anyway and has stayed in the trailer most of the weekend.

Our fist night David and I walked around the park and it was dark because the lights were far apart and not very bright anyway. As we strolled along the dirt trail talking about nothing much except going fishing in the morning, I noticed David was walking much closer to me than usual. Then, as if in a confession, he looked up into my face with your eyes and said to me in a low voice, almost like a whisper, that he was afraid of the dark as he slipped his little arm through mine. How can a grandmother's heart burst with pride and break, all at the same time?

He is so sweet, Paul, and so much like you were at his age. To walk with him is to stride in your footsteps; to hold him is to feel you close. He seems to worry about things that I find silly but, in his mind, they are important to him, so much like you did when you were his age.

Tonight he is worried about alligators coming out of the water, and in his irrational fears I could see your overactive imagination springing to life in your little boy. We walked close and I told him I would never let anything bad happen to him. I love his sensitivity, just like you, though I wonder how seriously he takes my promise.

I promised the same to you on many an occasion…

Morning came with a big red glow in the Gulf-of-Mexico and we were ready to go fishing. We fished for more than two hours, casting our lines off the pier at the far end, away from most of the other families that were fishing there. Finally David looked at me and said, quite wisely I thought, "This dumb old fake bait wouldn't catch a thing." We agreed to go back to the trailer, check on grandpa and have lunch. After lunch we would go into the little town nearby and pick up some live bait and then for sure our luck would change.

As we walked back down the pier toward our trailer we spotted a father fishing off the bank of the river with his two little girls. They seemed to be catching something so we walked over to see what they'd hauled in. Sure enough they were catching all different kinds of little fish. The father told us to use little pieces of hot dogs and we would catch something. I thanked him and we were soon on our way.

As we walked back to the trailer, however, David seemed unusually quiet. I wondered if he was remembering times that you took him fishing; wondered if his little heart was hurting as much as mine from seeing a Dad with his kids having so much fun, but in his usual way he never said a word about it.

Paul, I know I could never be a substitute for you but I hope in some small way that I can help fill your void in David's life.

After lunch David couldn't wait to go to the store to buy some hot dogs and then go fishing again. We got the hot dogs and off we went to the far end of the pier to fish some more. I'll say this: your boy is quite the little taskmaster, and I won't even ask where he got *that* from. As I sat on the park bench behind him my job was to bait his hook every time it was empty.

Once I tried to give him instructions on how to cast his new pole, and he seemed indignant when he quickly let me know that you had taught him how to do it. I didn't know whether to be proud or hurt. I quickly shrugged it off; such moments are precious and not to be wasted borrowing trouble where it doesn't exist.

Sure enough, that helpful father was right: every time David would cast his line into the water, he would get a bite after only a few minutes. He was catching catfish, or some other baitfish, so now he was having a good time and wanted me to take a picture of every single catch. (A born ham, just like his father!!!)

Once he snagged the bottom of the river and was dragging the line along the bottom, he thought he had caught himself a whopper and was sure it was nothing short of a whale. Because he had to put so much muscle into bringing in whatever it was on the end of his line, he told me to get the net ready because "this was going to be a keeper."

I could tell by the way the line was pulling that he had most likely snagged some weeds or something else. When he finally got the line in he had snagged an old tin can filled with mud and seawater. I laughed so hard because he had the cutest smile on his face, standing there holding up his catch, this rusty tin can, and still he wanted me to take a picture of it as well. I couldn't help but smile to myself as I took the prize picture of the day and knew that you would have wanted the same.

The afternoon wore on but he never tired of casting his line out so as long as they lasted I kept baiting his hook with hot dogs. His fun, his joy, his laughter was yours today and I missed you so much. Once when David cast out his line, almost to himself, he said, "this one's for you Dad." My heart stopped; I couldn't breathe and tears came to my eyes. I had a hard time trying to compose myself for a little while, but was finally in control of my emotions by the time we headed back to the trailer.

After checking on Dad and cleaning up, David and I headed for the Wildlife Park to go to the zoo. I just love watching David in new environments; he is so eager to learn and is so curious about everything. He was amazed at the size of the gators and was most excited about going down into the viewing area to get up close and personal with the massive manatees. It seemed like his eyes—your eyes, Paul—couldn't take it all in at once.

As I lay in bed tonight I wondered how David felt seeing that Dad fishing with his kids today. David loved going fishing with you and I just hope he never forgets those times that he *did* go fishing with you. My prayer tonight is a simple one:

Lord, please don't let the world and life desensitize this precious little boy. How blessed we are to have him so close and to be involved in his life. Thank you, Lord. Amen...

9

Recognition

+

November, 2003

Another name recognition for my hero: When Birgit and I were told that a certain facility in Orlando wanted to rename their building after you, I never did catch their name, I was pleased but not impressed.

At least, not at first.

Birgit and I were invited to Orlando to see firsthand what this was all about since Lisa was the one in touch with this center to help make the decisions. The whole time Lisa had kept us up to date as to what was going on, but still I really wasn't impressed. I guess I was just tired of bringing back so many memories and opening the wounds of war again. At first, I didn't even want to get involved.

Then the facility in Orlando sent a car for us and we met the man in charge, Larry Ziock; what a nice man he was. Subtly, my mind began to change. The name of the building we went to was THE ARMY SIMULATION TRAINING CENTER; what a mouthful. Why, I wondered, did the Army always have to make everything so complicated? This two story building was like many others in the area, boasting names on the outside that didn't really say what went on inside.

So what was so special about this building in Orlando anyway?

The Army Simulation Center was so much more then I could ever have imagined it to be. After touring the center and seeing what type of up-to-date and cutting edge technology was being used to train our soldiers, I was impressed and knew right away that this was the perfect building to be named after you.

After our tour, Larry had taken us into the conference room where there were drawings of what the building would look like and all that was being done in the conference room to honor you. When the cloth was taken off the picture of you that would one day be on the outside of this very special building, I felt your presence in that room at that very moment and knew you were there giving your stamp of approval. The plans were there in black and white, the date set for the ceremony, approval all around and once again I had to say that your sister Lisa had done a superb job since she was the one in charge of it all, along with Larry of course.

You would be so proud of her, Paul. Lisa has once again honored you in a way no one else could. Birgit and I were to supply memorabilia for the shadow boxes that were being built in the conference room.

For my contribution I wanted whoever would look into the shadow boxes to not only see the awesome soldier that you were but I also wanted them to get to know the great *man* you were. Immediately, I went home and got started.

First I collected pictures of your childhood, then I tore my albums apart and the finished product showed you in all different stages and ages, each tenderly snapped photograph depicting the many sides of you. Finally, I pasted them all on large poster board, in collage form. Since I had bought you so many of your collected eagles I wanted to include a few of them as well.

It seemed only right…

Birgit brought so many of your medals and awards, including a small toy motorcycle just like your real one, and other things that were important to her. I felt so proud of you, so good about what the center was doing by naming the building after you, but even with the slight diversion in the end there was really nothing that makes me feel good about your death.

Now I have learned that you have been nominated to receive the Congressional Medal-of-Honor, but time will tell. Your story and the events of your actions have been told and retold, and newspapers all over the country are calling you a hero, and rightfully so.

But I think about that day and can't help but wonder if you really knew what you were doing or were you just running on high adrenaline. I know the truth in my heart; you were so brave, Paul. I know that you did what you had to do; it was God's plan all along. I am still so angry that God chose you, though.

Why not someone else? Will I ever not be angry and sad? I hate my life knowing I won't ever see you again here. Even these celebrations, where men of valor and importance honor you with tears in their eyes and medals and even buildings, and still the bitterness ruins them for me.

Your actions that day didn't surprise any of us; we just go on wishing it hadn't been you.

Dedication Ceremony
for the
Sergeant First Class Paul Ray Smith
Simulation & Training Technology Center

24 September 1969 - 4 April 2003

November 7, 2003

U.S. Army
Research, Development & Engineering Command
(RDECOM)

12423 Research Parkway Orlando, Florida 32826

Dedication Ceremony
Agenda

Time	Program Events
1400-1445	Fallen Soldier Dedication Ceremony
	Presentation of Colors- *11th Engineering Battalion*
	National Anthem - *Sergeant First Class Henry Owens*
	Invocation - *Chaplain Kevin Sears, 3d Infantry Division*
	Host Welcome - *Major General John Doesburg, Commanding General, Research, Development & Engineering Command*
	State of Florida Keynote Address - *Lieutenant Governor Toni Jennings*
	Dedication Keynote - *Brigadier General José Riojas, Assistant Division Commander for Support, 3d Infantry Division*
	Combat Engineer Keynote - *Brigadier General Randal Castro, U.S. Army Corp of Engineers*
	Soldiers Address - *Command Sergeant Major Gary Coker, Engineer Brigade, 3d ID*
	Family Address - *Mrs. Lisa DeVane, Sister*
	Picture Presentation To Mrs. Paul Smith- *Major General Doesburg*
	Family Placement of "Paver Stones" & Memorial Site Unveiling
	Retreat - *3d Infantry Division Color Guard*
	Army Song and 3d ID Song - *Played by 3d ID Band*
445-1500	Ceremony Conclusion - *Major General Doesburg*
500-1630	Reception - *Soldiers Conference Room & Tours Inside*

Birgit, Janice, Lisa,

Your unyielding strength, courage and devotion, inspired us to achieve this day!

We Shall Never Forget!

Sincerely,
"The Committee"

10

Dedication Day—Orlando, Florida

◆

November 7, 2003

We arrived at the center around 8:00 A.M. on dedication day and were escorted into the conference room where last minute details were being ironed out. It was a very auspicious occasion. Everything was spit shined and ready for the ceremony to begin, but before it did we met with Major Generals, Brigadier Generals, Sergeant Majors, Captains, the Lieutenant Governor, dignitaries and the ever present press.

I think every news channel in Florida was standing around, along with some I had never even heard of before. Your friends, your boys, bands and civilians alike were all waiting outside and it was time for the family to be escorted out to where there was a bright white canopy set up for us to sit under.

As we were escorted out I felt like I was moving on a cloud. I was barely able to talk and my only clear sense was my eyesight. As I looked out over the crowd I was taken aback by the sheer size of it all and wondered if they all knew you. I noticed that the sky was the most brilliant blue with big puffy white clouds scattered randomly; it was warm out with hardly a breeze to spare. We reached the canopy and all the chairs were facing the building, which had a large blue cloth hanging from the roof to hide your image. It was only then that I noticed the strangest detail: each chair had a box of Kleenex and a bottle of water at its feet. The ceremony started with Reveille being played.

The first American flag to fly on the new flagpole outside the newly renamed SFC Paul Ray Smith Simulation and Training Facility was being brought out, its somber march no match for the somber music. The soldiers that were marching toward us all looked so very young and so smart in dress uniform. The soldier that was holding the flag had his head ever so slightly bent forward, as if in prayer. He was not alone.

His hands held the flag so tenderly against his chest, it all looked so surreal and I thought of other flags folded in this same way: The flag off of my father's casket, folded and given to my mother so tenderly, the same flag you and Dad put up the pole on the river. The flag that was presented to me at your funeral in Hinesville, Georgia.

So much death.

Would I ever look at an American flag the same way again?

The soldiers unfolded the flag and it was raised up the flagpole; once at the top it seemed to hesitate and then a soft breeze caught it and our beautiful stars and strips unfurled ever so slowly, as if choreographed to do so at the behest of some unseen hand.

Was it yours?

The presentation of our colors and the National Anthem was sung, the invocation was evoked by Chaplain Keven Sears of the 3rd Infantry division. Then the host speaker, Major General John Doesburg, welcomed everyone and said that this was a day to celebrate your memory and recognize a hero and his legacy that would live on forever. Even though it was not to be a sad ceremony, somehow I didn't see it as a celebration.

How could I celebrate the fact that you had been killed and I would never get hugs, kisses, cards, and stories from you ever again? I just wasn't in a celebratory mood.

Can you ever forgive me?

Representing the state of Florida was the next speaker, Lieutenant Governor Toni Jennings. She said that she wanted this "…to be a day to remember all service men and women from the first wars to present, and to never forget that it is with the blood of these fine men and women that makes our country what is right." She said it was "fitting to rename this center after you." She never knew you or met you but no truer words were ever spoken. She called you a "hero among heroes" and said that you were "an inspiration to all."

Brigadier General, Jose Riojas Dogface soldier, 3rd Infantry Division spoke, saying: "Rock of the Marne," before he continued, explaining that "…the fight for freedom continues today and if we don't fight the terrorist overseas, we one day may have to fight them here in our own country."

He went on to say that "men like you knew this and that is why you did not let your fear of risk sway your quest for a mission accomplished." He said that you were a "patriot that was willing to sacrifice your tomorrows to ensure that we would have a lifetime of freedom."

He called you a "soldier with a warrior's spirit." He said that your "legacy was in your training, mentoring, and your leadership; you were the role model of a hero. You gave everything for your country. Rock of the Marne."

Brigadier General Randal Castro spoke next, comparing you with the Knights of the Round Table, and said that in any other time you would have been one of the Three Musketeers! (I silently laughed and wondered what your brother Tony thought of that.) He continued talking and said that while talking to your boys, they told him that you were a hero everyday and you would have argued that it was your boys who were the real heroes.

A prouder mother you could not find but even I was taken aback by the next speaker because I felt that this was a man that really knew you and what you stood for. Command Sergeant Major Gary Coker told us that he had served with you in Desert Storm, explaining that he knew "you were a rising star even then." My heart was aching for this man because I was seeing so much pain from my loss present in his eyes. I could see that there had been a very real connection between the two of you.

He made us all laugh when he told us that he got assigned to where you were and he said he knew he "was in for a wild ride." He also said you were not the average senior NCO. He related that "...he loved arguing with you because you argued for the sake of arguing, but always argued for the right reason, for the young warriors and your boys."

He challenged us all to "look into the eyes of your boys and we would see SFC Paul Ray Smith." He called you "the ultimate Sapper, Leader, Warrior and Senior NCO." He called you a hero and said you should be honored for deeds done. He said you "died more then a soldier's death, you died a hero's death. HOOAH!"

As I listened to this giant of a man I made a note to be sure to speak with him after the ceremony. I knew that this was a man who surely had great stories to tell about you, and somehow I felt very close to this man even though I'd never even met him before that day.

Then your sister Lisa walked to the podium to once again be the spokesperson for our family. Standing tall, proud and beautiful, wearing your smile and holding back the tears, she could have done no better as she talked about you as a man, about your goodness, and how much you "will be missed."

She said you were not only a "professional soldier bearing the finest and bravest traits of this profession, but you were a kind and loving husband, a much loved and respected father, a fine son and brother and a good man at the core of your soul."

She went on to say "what a privilege and honor it is to have this building named after you." She said, with a falter in her voice, that after the ceremony was over and everyone went home, "for the Smith family the battle is not over. Our family would live out our lives, with a missing father, husband, son and brother at our family dinners. That your rugged smile would no longer be a part of our family pictures."

She also talked about your love for your troops. She told the story of how when one of your soldier's wives was in the hospital one Christmas and was unable to provide Christmas for their children how you and Birgit gave them a Christmas that year. It was just one of the many silent acts of kindness that no one knew about till after your death. (Although, secretly, I was less than surprised.)

She told another story about one of your soldier's children who had been admitted to a hospital after unexpectedly becoming very ill. How you would drive one hour every night into Savanna, Georgia to the hospital to support this soldier and his wife until their daughter was well enough to come home. She then read parts of your last letter home to your father and I.

She spoke about the tremendous responsibility you felt for your boys' safety and how you were willing to give all to ensure their safe return home. Lisa concluded with a poem that had been sent to her after your death, it read:

The Band of Brotherhood

As a brilliant hot sun broke over the pristine mountains of old El Paso, 24 September 1969, Paul Ray Smith's glorious destiny began.

We were not there...but as brothers we watched.

As Paul Ray traversed the sunny hot streets of childhood to manhood in old Tampa.

We were not there...but as brothers we watched.

As Paul Ray firmly raised his right hand entering America's army at old Fort Leonardwood on a bright hot sunny 1989 day.

We were not there...but as brothers we watched closely.

As a young soldier with beads of sweat trickling from his forehead to dog tags and hot sand beating hard into his skin, Paul Ray bravely faced his first combat in old Operation Desert Storm.

We were not there…but as brothers we watched closely.

As clouds grew dark, eight foot waves rose high above the Gulf-of-Mexico and family became sickened with fear, Paul Ray with only a key repaired the hot electrical system of the capsizing boat. Saving his precious cargo.

We were not there…but as brothers we watched.

As a new Sergeant Paul Ray stood steadfast in the cold bitter wind swept ruins of old Kosavo and proudly reenlisted before comrades and generals.

We were not there…but as brothers we watched closely.

As a brilliant hot sun broke over the pristine Tigris Euphrates River in old Baghdad, 4 April 2003 and as Paul Ray's destiny began to be fulfilled…

This time as brothers…we were there.

As Paul Ray's final mission came to a glorious close we reached out comforting our brother with soft words.

Sapper 7.

You have…my brother…done your soldier duty…you have my brother…given your family honor…you have my brother…ultimately served your country.

Duty…honor…country, and now my brother it is time to go, not raging into the old dark, but rather passing through a brilliant young pristine sunlight of life.

Yes, my brother, it is time to join us, leave forever-eternal old guard.

The Marne band of brotherhood.

Welcome home, my brother.

Signed,

Forever Army soldier

The speeches were over, and the center had made a courtyard with a beautiful fountain with white doves that adorned it, and a brick floor where there were spaces for extra bricks. Each family member had the opportunity to have something engraved on the stone pavers before they were set in the ground.

The family was escorted to a table that was set up next to the building with the stone pavers resting on top. Birgit went first, her stone paver read, "You're still the one, love always, your wife." Then David picked his up with the words that read, "You're the best Dad, David." Jessica's stone paver was in German, with one word that you used to say to her often, "BASTA! (meaning "Stay out of trouble, the end") Love, Jessica." Dad's paver read, "You're always my hero, Dad." As I picked up my paver, mine too only had one word on it: "HOOAH, love Mom."

I'm still not sure what exactly "hooah" means but for me it means, "job well done," it means "the best of the best," and Paul, you *were* the best of the best. Tony came next and his paver said, "Our brother, our hero, your brother, Tony." I still can't believe that Lisa was able to get so much on her stone. It read, "You're still an inspiration, I will cherish all you gave me, every day. Your devoted sister, Lisa." The last paver only has one word on it, not even signed. It reads, "HERO!"

The day had turned hotter than expected and we were all ready to go back in where it would be cool. As the family was facing the building waiting for the unveiling of the new name Birgit stepped forward and cut the ribbon that held the cloth down. The cloth rose and your image came into view.

Paul, it was literally breathtaking. At this point I still had my composure in tact but then your song, "Proud to be an American" started to play. The posture that I had all day cracked and the tears started to flow. As a family we cried together, held each other for comfort, as a family I suddenly realized that, now, this is all we could do.

As we walked back into the relief of the air-conditioned conference room I thought about your sister's speech. When it was over, I couldn't have been more proud of her. As she spoke about who you were and how much you would be missed there was no doubt in anyone's mind how much she respected and loved you. Her tribute to you was so wonderful and I know you were watching her every move and hanging on her every word, and yes, she is right: it *will* be a much sadder world with you not in it.

The conference room was refreshing, shiny and new and your heart and soul were there on the walls for all to see. What had been a ceremony dissolved quickly into a photo opportunity so the day could be recorded for posterity. Paul, you would have been proud of us; we all behaved as the shutters snapped and the flashbulbs ignited, giving the room that bore your name a staccato glow of bright, white light.

The pictures were taken, the press was finally done with their questions and all I wanted to do was go watch David play inside the simulations. Paul, it was just like seeing you there and I couldn't help but wonder if David would choose the same path as you did. In my heart I pray he won't but it wouldn't surprise me if he did. If it happens to be true, I know that we will support him in the same way that we supported you.

Our loss was the country's gain...

At the end of the day I walked outside to sit quietly and reflect, to just gaze up at your picture being so thankful that they used one of my favorite pictures of you. All day I felt as if you were there with me. I could actually feel your presence in everything I did and saw. I couldn't believe what had started out as just another tribute to my son turned out to be such an honor and life-affirming experience. Now I felt really good about this building and what it was all about and in my heart I knew that you, too, approved of what went on here today.

I can't help but be so proud of you, Paul. As I sit and look up into the eyes of your picture I can see the smile you always gave me, and I know that this building that now wears not only your name but your image as well is the epitome of you.

My son; my hero.

Today I did find a little bit of closure, although it still is no consolation for me. I wish I could make this all go away and have you home instead of this wonderful building that is stone cold, so much like my heart has become.

I wonder, will there ever come a time that I am not sad or lonely for you?

11

New Journeys

✦

November 18, 2003

Paul, even in death you have taken me on journeys I never thought I would take. I never thought I would see New York proper, and I never really thought about seeing it in the first place; it wasn't on my top ten list of thing to do.

The Montel Williams Show was doing a program on fallen soldiers so Birgit, Jessica, Lisa and I were invited to be on the show along with other families. Since Lisa had been the spokesperson for the family, she and Jessica were the only ones that actually appeared on the show. Birgit and I stayed in the background and, trust me, from what I saw that day that was just fine with me.

I met some of the other guests for the day; we talked and cried together and watched the show from backstage. I always loved watching Montel on the tube, I felt that he was a very caring person; I have never watched him again since that day. As I watched closely from backstage I felt him short of attention for his guests, and not very interested in what they had to say. Lisa and Jessica were the last to go on with him and I didn't feel that he spent enough time listening to Lisa. In fact, I felt that he cut her short and was not very sincere at all in his responses. I think he could care less if you were the only soldier to be nominated for the Medal-of-Honor; I got the feeling he really didn't care if he did this show or not.

The following day would be our last day in New York so Lisa and I woke up early. Jessie preferred to sleep so we headed out to see New York proper; with the temperature just slightly cool, making our walk very pleasant as we took in the sights.

I know that we must have walked at least ten miles that day, and I so enjoyed being with Lisa were it not for the fact that our every thought was consumed with sadness over you. We tried to soldier on, as you would say, and went through Bryant Park, where I saw my very first dog park. I wanted to just linger for a while and watch all the dogs running and playing. Lisa, along with the other people assembled there, thought I was strange and kept looking at me as if to say, "Haven't you ever seen a dog park before?" Well, the truth was that, no I hadn't.

We walked to Ground Zero; the realization that this is the place where it all started rendered me speechless. I couldn't help but think that if this tragedy hadn't occurred you might still be alive and with those thoughts came the solid feeling of pain and loss with which I've become so familiar. Not only for you but for those lost in the towers and the sadness and pain for those other families was so real I could have cut the feelings with a knife. It is so hard to put into words the black void I feel. But I will try, Paul.

For you I will try anything if I think it might help...

We continued to walk in silence, both ambling side by side but in fact alone with our own thoughts about Ground Zero; soon we were in the financial district and yet I still couldn't lose the profound feeling of sadness that had come over me. The sights and sounds of New York had somehow lost their flavor.

We rested in a park and I marveled at the New Yorkers we met while we sat there. We asked several people where St. Michael's Church was and even though they had lived there for between five and twenty years, no one could tell us. I just laughed; later we headed out on foot to see the Statue of Liberty.

Our walk was brisk and we were both feeling a bit tired by then but knowing that we would have to return to the hotel soon because our plane would soon be leaving to bring us home once again made us try to use up whatever precious time we had left. With time limited we walked as close to "the lady" as we could get; the sight of her made me feel so American, I wish we could have taken the ferry over to Ellis Island. Oh well, maybe next time I'm in New York.

As I sat on the plane on my way home I thought how I would really like to return one day. There was so much I would have loved to see. I really wanted to go to the Statue, Central Park, China Town and so much more. I made a little promise to myself that one day, God willing, I would return.

Grandmother Died This Month

I didn't think that she was going to die and, the truth is, I just wasn't ready for her to go quite yet. I know that is so selfish of me but I needed her, just like I needed you. Mom always listened to me, even if she couldn't quite comprehend what my feelings were at the time. In these later years that seemed too short she was always there for me. I hope that during the last years she was here I made her happy. At least I know that I tried. I'm going to miss her so much. Another death this year; this makes three family members in one year. I wonder what God is trying to tell me. I am so tired, Paul.

So tired of death and sadness and loneliness and pain…

You know she always talked about you and how good you were to her. You never forgot to go see her first when you would come home; she loved you so much for that. I hope you were there when she crossed over. Funny how we never think that our children will go on before us; it's not right that a parent should bury or outlive their children.

I'm so glad that Birgit bought our house; she said that it is where you always seemed to be happy and was where the family came for the holidays or just to be together as a family. She says she feels close to you there, and it makes me happy because we live so close now and I will be able to see the kids often. I'm glad she feels this way, for I felt so close to you there, too.

In my mind's eye I would see you coming down the hall, in the kitchen sneaking grape leaves out of the pot on the stove. I saw you in the pool with the kids and always could picture your smiling face. Maybe too close for me, as my mind's eye won't let you go, but then it probably never will no matter where I live.

Dad and I are settled in our villa and it suits us well. I think you would like it and agree that it suits us. With Dad being so sick it is the perfect space for me to take care of him. I wonder if Dad's recovery is so slow because he is grieving inside for you and can't come to terms with your death. In an e-mail to Birgit you told her that Dad was occupying a lot of your thoughts in those last days. I, too, wondered that if you hadn't been so worried about Dad you might have been saved.

I am so grateful for this journal, where I can write to you in spite of the fact that you will never answer. I do a lot of my crying here for you; something that Dad finds hard to do. We are getting settled in the villa although my body doesn't seem as convinced because it is always in so much pain.

Will I ever wake up and not have heartache?

December 15, 2003

I woke up this morning to news that I didn't expect to hear this year. Dad was watching the news and as I walked into the room he said, "Saddam has been captured." I almost couldn't believe what I was hearing. My eyes stayed glued to the television set and my body was paralyzed to the spot, so Dad brought me a cup of coffee and made me sit. I wasn't even aware of the fact that I hadn't moved since entering the living room.

As I watched the news my feelings were of joy and relief; I had feelings of celebration as well. Then I had feelings of anger and hate. I cried for joy and I cried for sadness; I cried for gain and I cried for loss.

I went out and bought a newspaper today, and on the front page was a picture of the devil; his name was Saddam Hussein. Will this make a difference? Will the killing stop now? To date our military has lost four hundred sixty two men and women; you were the ninety-eighth one to die in the desert. That was just on our side, but I can't help but wonder about the Iraqi people, the innocent ones that didn't want a war in their country. What about all the children that have been killed, the ones with no voice?

I don't understand war; I hate the sight of this man. Will he get what he deserves for the lives that he took in such a brutal way? And even if he does, will it make a difference in that country? Will the killing stop then? (Probably not.) Will his country ever have peace? Then again, will ours?

All questions that will remain unanswered, now and in the future. Will God forgive me for hating this man so and wanting to see him die? What has happened to me? What about 'love the neighbor'? What kind of a concept is this? How can I turn the other cheek? An eye for an eye? How can I not feel this way; this is not what I have been taught.

Emotions chase each other inside my head till I think it may explode. How do I deal with all of this? God help me, please.

December 25, 2003
Our First Christmas Without You

Christmas at George Island in the Panhandle of Florida and I didn't expect to be here but as midnight rolls around, we arrive only several hours before dawn. The house is quiet but it won't be for long.

Santa has come and so have we.

I am so glad that Lisa and Bradley rented the beach house for a family Christmas. I know that the main reason was so Birgit and the kids would not have to spend their first Christmas without you alone. Not that they would spend it alone but it's not the same as having the family all together.

Dad and I hadn't planned to go since it was a seven-hour drive from home and Dad still wasn't doing all that well. At the last minute on Christmas Eve we jumped in the car and drove all night just to be there when the kids woke up and I'm so glad we did. Christmas just wouldn't have been any fun without being with all the friends, family and, of course, most of all—the grandchildren.

The beach house was a four story, one million dollar home with a swimming pool and an elevator inside; to say it was quite something would be an under statement. This is one of the many homes that Lisa had worked her magic in with her graphic art talent. Downstairs were French doors to the patio where the pool was located. On that wall there was a complete scene of a tropical forest with palms and birds in the trees; the colors were so alive you had to touch the wall to know it wasn't real.

In the bathroom on this floor it appeared that sea grass was coming out of the woodwork and little green frogs from behind the sink. Lisa's magic was present on each floor; if you looked closely as you walked up to the second floor, in the corner of a window sill sat another little frog. There was a method to her silliness; she had painted a total of twelve little frogs all in secret hiding places. Whoever found all twelve frogs got a special surprise. I could almost see you looking for the frogs before the kids would find them; that was your way: silly, just like Lisa.

On the main floor Lisa had put up a Christmas tree, all in red, white and blue. I added my ornament that told everyone that you were spending Christmas with Jesus this year. On the fourth floor where Dad and I had our own bedroom with another master bath we could see the Gulf-of-Mexico and the beach. The weather was a bit cold for the beach but you know how I draw strength from the sea, and knowing how much you would have loved being there, I somehow felt very close to you as I looked out over the water.

I had sad moments of loneliness and still disbelief, longing to see you playing with the kids on the beach, but in my heart you *were* there and I *did* see you. Everyone was having such a great time, the kids being kids and all us adults trying not to miss you so.

The last evening we were there we all went down to the beach. I loved watching Lisa and Bradley with Greyson and Olivia Rae playing on the sand, then singing "Happy Birthday, Jesus" with sparklers in hand. Wonderful pictures for our album but, of course, missing your "rugged smile" as your sister called it; your beautiful smile, and David's smile now.

As the sun was setting it was getting cold and the wind was starting to whip up but I didn't mind. I felt so peaceful. Lisa, Brad, and the kids headed back to the house for some hot chocolate and Dad also had to go back in, but I couldn't leave, not just yet. The sky was turning a cotton candy pink and I knew right then that I wouldn't leave the beach for a long time, no matter how cold it got.

As the sky went from pink to orange and then a light red I couldn't take my eyes off of it. The sky was turning a light purple. I had never seen this color in the sky before and I was mesmerized. All of a sudden, just as if God had turned on a night-light, the sky turned a deep purple with streaks of light red and orange. I was so glad I had my camera with me; no one would have believed what I saw without proof. I wondered if you had a hand in painting the sky for me tonight; I thought of you for a long time after the sun set.

Dad and I are leaving in the morning, as he has to be back to work on Monday. Poor guy, he had no time to rest over the holiday. I know he agreed to come just for me and I do feel a little selfish but I really needed to be with the kids this year. I'll make it up to him. Your sister Lisa really did make a wonderful Christmas for everyone this year; you know she did it for you.

A New Year will soon be here, a New Year without you, another year to just get through.

12

A New Year

✦

January 1, 2004

After we came home from the beach house I fell into a heavy depression. It hit me unexpectedly—I thought I was doing so well. I was so bad I didn't even want to get out of bed; it seemed that no matter what I did I just couldn't pull myself together. I'd never felt like that before. I'd heard people talk about depression and always wondered why they couldn't just "get over it." Now I knew. And how...

On December 30th I called my sister-in-law Barbara in Albany New York and asked if she wanted company and would she like to drive into New York City to see the ball drop on New Years Eve in Times Square. Barbara's beloved husband Max had died in June of 2003, so I wasn't sure what her answer would be.

I guess she knew that we both needed something different to start the New Year so she said two words: "come on." I couldn't believe that I was on the computer booking us airline tickets and a hotel in downtown New York only blocks from Time Square. As I confirmed the reservations I thought, "What in the world was I thinking?"

Too late now; the deed done, I called Barb and she said she would pick us up at the Albany Airport. Now to tell Dad what I did. As he walked in the door that evening I could see how tired and worn out he was from the drive to George Island and once again in less than two weeks I saw my ugly selfish self had given no thought to him. When I told Dad what I had done, he was not upset at all but I wasn't sure that it was only a façade that he wore on his face.

I packed and we left on the 30th of December 2003. Talk about doing things at the last minute! After we had arrived in Albany and spent an evening at Barb's, I could see how tired the trip had made Dad. The next afternoon we took off for New York City, arriving at the hotel around dinnertime late in the afternoon. After dropping off our overnight bags we headed out to find a little restaurant close to the hotel, as Dad seemed to be fading fast. It was New Year's Eve and I wanted Dad to join Barb and I in the nighttime festivities.

After dinner it took all Dad had to walk the several blocks back to the hotel, where he decided that he would watch the ball drop from the easy chair by the window. As I watched him ease himself into the chair, I felt guilty for having dragged him all this way when what he really needed was more rest.

We only had three days but it was something I needed to do; to start the year off on a positive note and with Barbara I did. I knew I still had to come home to all the memories of last year but for once in my life I just wanted to be in the moment and not have to think about tomorrow. Tomorrow we would go home and the New Year would begin. For now I just wanted to stay up late and watch the country go on in its foolishness, pretending that bright lights and funny hats and noisemakers could push back the endless night that was promised to us all.

Lord, protect this family and give us more faith. Faith to believe that your will be done. Amen.

January 25, 2004

A reporter for the St. Petersburg *Times* newspaper here in Florida, Alex Leary, has done an eight-page special report about you, not only in the newspaper but the St. Pete *Times* has made an interactive web site out of the article as well.

Alex had been interviewing the family, talking to the military about you and what you did in Iraq to warrant you being nominated for the Medal-of-Honor. Paul, he did such a great job. He collected information from all kinds of different sources and made this very personal to anyone that read it. The interactive web site is unbelievable; there is a guest book so whoever visits the site can make comments about it.

Every time I visit the guest book it just blows me away to read what people have to say about the article and, more importantly, about you. People as far away as England, Canada and all over the United States, young and old, every profession you can imagine come and visit. And they write, Paul. Oh, do they write. It's like this journal; they all have something to say and, in a way, you've brought that out of them. Out of us.

Out of me...

They write to thank Alex for the outstanding work he did on the article, they write the family and express their most heartfelt condolences and all thank you and bless you for what you did.

I can see you sitting up there on that cloud with that sideways smirk saying, "Come on Mom, I was just doing my job and you know it."

Well son, all I can say is: "Job well done; you're the man!"

February 2, 2004

The family went to Jessica's school this evening. The Renaissance of Fine Arts Academy was putting on a performance, one of several they do each year to show the parents how talented the kids that go there are. I must say I was quite impressed; you could really tell the difference between the students that are at the school for the fine arts and the ones that go there just because it is a private school.

I saw some very talented young adults, and as I watched I wondered which of them would one day be famous. Jessie was on stage twice this evening, both times with a singing group. She wore her beautiful blue prom gown; she looks so much older than her real age. As I watched her perform I remembered the very first time I saw her; she was so young with light brown curly hair, sparkling big brown eyes and so, so sweet.

It was Christmas day at Fort Benning, Georgia, where you had brought your new wife and daughter to the states for the very first time. Dad and I decided to surprise you and Birgit that year. We called you early Christmas morning from the hotel to wish you a "Happy Christmas," and even though we woke the whole house up we didn't tell you we were there in Georgia.

When we arrived at your door a short time later, Poinsettia plant in one hand and presents in the other when you opened the door, you didn't seem that surprised that we drove most of the night to be with you. You *did* know me too well. You looked tired and sleepy with that sweet baby doll face I loved so much. That was the day we met our daughter-in-law for the first time and our beautiful little Jessica. Birgit was so shy and so fat with our little baby David. And Jessica was such a sweet and happy little angel.

You cooked dinner that Christmas and all our prayers that day were ones of thankfulness for your family and your happiness. That day I sat back and watched you as a father and a husband for the first time. I was thrilled to see you happy and to know that you had reached the goals you always talked about.

It made me so happy to just sit and watch as you tossed Jessie around like a little rag doll and her laughter filled the air. Dad and I knew that you weren't very happy over the fact that we had bought Jessie too many presents but in your quiet way you said nothing out loud, although your eyes really "gave us hell."

February 2004
Valentine's Day

May 14, 19 78

Dear Mother:
   I love you very much!

HAPPY Mother's Day.

     Love,
     Paul

The only one of my kids to give me a card this year was Birgit and David. It only served to remind me that you never forgot my Birthday, Christmas, Mother's Day or Valentines Day. Would you believe that I still have your very first Valentines card you gave me? You made it in school and I remember how proud of it you were. I dug that card out today and I laughed because of the mis-spelled words but loved what it said. I always loved getting cards and letters from you, even as an adult, you couldn't spell. Oh well, at least you came by it honestly because, as you know, without a dictionary I am lost.

David called me to wish me Happy Valentines Day; he is so you Paul, you would be so proud of him. I'm trying really hard not to say things like that to him because I don't want him to feel he has to live up to who you were. I want to help him know who he is and to know that he is great in himself, no matter what he chooses in life.

I am taking Jessica to see Cirque Du Soleil on Sunday. It's so hard to plan things with her; she is such a teenager with her own agenda. I want the time we spend together to be special because soon she will be too old to hang out with her Grandma—or so she will think.

Sunday

Jessie and I went to lunch in St. Pete today and then to the Cirque Du Soleil. I loved watching her face; she is such a pretty girl and so smart. I watched as her face would light up, and then it seemed like she was concentrating so hard on one aspect of what she was seeing and a small smile would slowly form and then some real laughter. I enjoyed my day with Jessie so much; she can be a lot of fun when she forgets that she must be serious, much too serious for her age. I hope that we can build a strong relationship together. I believe she will need a constant in her life and I hope that I can be that for her.

Jessica misses you, Paul, but rarely talks about you. I'm sure it is because it is still too painful for her. I try to open the door of conversation about you but she isn't ready yet. I wish she would talk; I think it could help her.

Oh well, all in her own time.

February 29, 2004
Strawberry Festival

Plant City, Florida

As the family piled into the car today to go to the Strawberry Festival I remembered how much you loved going; it was one of the festivals that you rarely ever missed.

As Dad drove I went back in time, and in my mind's eye I could see other years when you went with us as a family. You and Crissy always wanting to go early and stay as late as possible, never giving thought to the long ride home.

One year when we went to the festival, Michael Jackson's song *Thriller* was so popular, it seemed that every third song you heard either on the radio or on the midway that year was *Thriller*. I could see you and your sister Crissy dancing on the midway that year to that song, you were both acting so silly, but as I looked around I saw that it was no more so than any other teenager that was there.

When you got your driver's license it was you and Greg going to the Strawberry Festival—sometimes alone and sometimes with girls. Even then you were growing up too fast for my satisfaction. Then it was you, Birgit and the kids. You always loved going; it brought out the kid in you no matter how old you were.

I saw you more than once in David today; it made me sad, it also made me happy but most of all it made me miss you so much. Thank you for your son and all the wonderful memories I have of you through his beautiful, smiling face. I only wish I could have seen you more in the father role.

I know you were a great Dad, but I would have liked to have seen you in your tender moments with the kids. In my mind I can see you teaching Jessie how to work on the car; I can see you fishing with David and flea marketing with Birgit. I missed so much of your adult life.

Will I never have a day that I don't cry for the loss of you?

13

I Was With You

✦

March 15, 2004

One year ago today, the war that took you from us started. You were so brave, Paul. I'm sure you never even thought about your own safety, only that of the men you were taking with you. Just this once I wish you would have been selfish, but that just wasn't part of the person you were.

I have to believe that this was God's plan for you. Your men were so lucky to have had you to lead them; you did such a great job of teaching them what they needed to know. I know that there are some of them that fight the demons in their minds, the "if I would have, I should have, or just maybe" games. I wish I knew a way to take those demons away for them; I would if I could.

We, too, were so blessed to have had you in our lives for thirty-three wonderful years. It doesn't stop the pain or "the knowing," as your sister Lisa voiced. Your nieces, nephews, your namesake, your grandchildren and generations to come will never hear your stories or know how great a man you were, but we will be sure that they will hear of your greatness, your sacrifice for them.

One year ago today; I can't stop thinking about it. I know you must have worn that look of determination on this day one year ago. The same look you wore with me when you were a kid and I would say, "No!" You would smile with those eyes that told me that wasn't the right answer, your back would straighten and off you would go with that look of defiance and determination on your face. I see it even now. My heart is heavy but I find some comfort in knowing you are in the arms of the Lord and at home with your band of brothers.

March 16, 2004

We are making arrangements for the one-year anniversary of your death. I can't believe that it has been one year already. So much has happened and so many changes have taken place. We have given so many interviews that I know all the questions by heart but I don't want to smile anymore and I don't want to explain that it was your destiny.

We all continue to move forward in our own time frame, some of us slowly, some of us barely, but move on we must, just as you would want us to. I still find it hard to accept the fact that I will never see your face on this earth again. I still hear your voice telling me "not to worry" because "you are ready" and you "will be okay." You wanted me to believe this and, because you said it, I did.

I still kept the "what ifs" at bay because I knew that could never happen to you. I wonder what we would have said differently to each other if we had only known. I never really said good-bye to you, only "…watch your back, take care of business and hurry home to us."

I so believed you when you said that you would be okay and home soon. After a whole year spent thinking back on all that was said and done, I now believe that you knew in your heart that your destiny was close at hand, or that this was a bad one and you really weren't sure at all but didn't want to worry us.

Like Jesus knew his fate.

I don't really think that you thought about your fate on a conscious level but thinking back, I believe now that you did think about it because of the many stories I have heard about the different ways you said good-bye to different people. The things that you did that were so out of character for you. Paul, those are the things that make me believe that you did think of the "what ifs," after all.

I do know that it was your boys that were constant on your mind; you took such great care of them and did it most honorably. And your love for your family and country. What greater love was there? We found out, didn't we? You gave it all you had and you did it well.

Today, one year ago, was the last time Birgit heard your voice. I hear your voice everyday when you come to me and say, "Don't worry Mom, I'll be fine."

March 19, 2004

Another honor for your family to represent you and all soldiers, as we have been invited to ride in and be the guest of honor on a float in the Chasco Fiesta parade in our little town of New Port Richey, but a big parade it is, and a very big honor.

David is so funny; he thinks that because it is his birthday month it is for him alone. After I explained it to him, he said that the real reason was "even better."

March 20, 2004
Parade Day

We arrived around 10:00 and hung out until the parade started. The weather wasn't too hot—for a change—and a slight breeze made it even better. Your sister-in-law Janee came with the boys, and then there was Birgit, Jessie, David and me. As we watched while tons of beads were being loaded onto the float, a very large picture of you was put up and adorned the front of the float; suddenly music from a speaker on top started to play patriotic songs.

That is when Birgit and I had our moment of tears, hugs and our time for sadness; we both knew it was coming, it was only a matter of when. Then it was "all aboard" and the parade finally got underway. I loved watching the kids run around the float and throw the beads along the parade route; for them it must have felt like Mardi Gras! Along the parade route there were many veterans, all of whom stood at attention and saluted as our float passed.

Once again you couldn't help but be proud to be an American that day, not to mention becoming painfully aware of how connected we all really are at times like these. Our David had such a great time in the parade, throwing beads and just being a little boy today.

I see you in him everyday and I thank God for your being who you were.

April 3, 2004

Today was really hard on me. They say that sometimes too much information is not good; such was the case for me today.

You would think I'd be prepared. After all, I had seen all the pictures, read all the statements of the account, seen the animation of the war you fought and heard the actual tape recording of the last battle you fought. I have even seen the very spot where the desert sands drank your blood and your life ended.

Today in Baghdad it is April 4th, 2004; today I am there as if it was exactly one year ago. I am with you; I feel your fear and apprehension. I am walking in the hot desert sun and the sweat is rolling down my face. I feel your adrenaline pumping ever so quickly in your veins; I can see the determined look in your beautiful green eyes. I am there with you, son, seeing what you see.

I feel the blackness that has surrounded you. I know that you are no longer there in this tired shell; I feel your soul surrendering. I am here with you but you are gone, all that remains is my broken heart. I wish I could have taken your place, son; you had so much more living to do, so much more good to accomplish on this planet, but your life was in your Father's hands that day.

It doesn't seem fair to me that you should have gone instead of me.

It's been one year and I still can't believe you won't be coming home. My mind knows the truth; it's my heart that can't mend. Then again, maybe tomorrow I will start to mend. At least I know that one day I will breathe again.

But that will not be this day, I fear...

Today is the last day that I will wear the little gold star that tells everyone who sees it that I lost you; for me to wear it means that I honor your sacrifice. I will only wear it one more time and that will be the day that you are awarded the Medal-of-Honor. My grief journal will also come to an end today. It has helped me a lot but brings back the hurt every time I write in it.

It also helps me to never forget, but how could I ever do that? And it helps me to remember every detail of you that I may forget in old age. In my head I hear you telling me how to honor you, and you know that I will. David will be well taken care of. I pray that I will never let you and Birgit down.

I can still be a mother; and that is a debt I plan to honor...

April 4, 2004
Palm Sunday

I sat in my chair today, almost paralyzed with thoughts of you and what you must have gone through on that fateful day in that hot, barren, faraway desert. How you must have wanted for your mother that day; how you must have needed me. I wish I could have been there for you, Paul.

What am I saying?

I wish I could have taken your place instead...

As I sit here I still feel as if I am walking with you in the desert; my body feels clammy with sweat, the heat so intense it's as if salt is pouring into my eyes even as I write these mournful words.

The experience is intense and unsettling; the noise of battle that you must have had filling your ears now makes mine ring. My adrenaline is spiking, my blood is pounding and now it feels as if there is no air to breathe in this room. I am so tired; I have walked a million miles with you already. How many more shall we travel together in this way? I felt you die that day; you died for me and everyday I live I will honor the sacrifice you made and thank you for keeping me free.

I can never take my freedom for granted, ever again.

They say that "time heals all things," but I believe that some things are never healed by time...

As I dressed today I automatically reached for my gold star; now my dress is complete and I will honor you once again, today. My journal, well, I couldn't let this day go by without writing in it and remembering all of today without you in it.

As Dad and I pulled up into the drive at Birgit's house it looked like a convention of the "Gold Star Club," almost every car there had the gold star of the fallen hero on it, just another reminder that you would not be joining us. We had a family dinner; it was very nice, all family, friends and invited guests. It was wonderful seeing everyone; we talked, watched the kids play but not one of the adults would say why we were all gathered together again, we all knew.

Birgit had bought a black marble headstone with your face engraved on it; she had it placed under her bedroom window in the backyard. She says that her bed is on the other side of the wall and your engraved face will now face her as she sleeps, just like you did when you were here.

As we all stood in the backyard she slowly took the cloth off the stone for all to see. It is very black and shiny; quite lovely, in fact. I hope that it will bring her great comfort. I placed a white rose next to your memorial and said a prayer, a prayer for this family that is in such pain.

The stone is very lovely but unlike dear Birgit I don't need a reminder that you are no longer with us. I feel your absence every day; there is nothing that can make me feel that you are close, although I do hope that it helps her.

April 8, 2004

I continue to write. I suppose it makes me feel that I am still in contact with you. Of course, I know you will never write me back but that's okay. This journal is an outlet for my pain and sorrow; I do feel like you are nearer if I keep writing.

I keep wondering what your thoughts would be about this war if you were here today. This last week the fighting in Iraq has been the fiercest since Bush declared the war's "end." We are fighting the Sunni Muslims and the fast growing Shiites. There are so many dying each day; not only on our side but theirs as well. Women and small children, those poor innocents, where will this all end?

Will it ever end?

I can't help but be both transfixed and disgusted by the nightly news. I watch it all, my channels pre-programmed to the all-news stations. There are so many of them now, and when they're not showing actual stories of the war a ticker tape keeps me constantly updated at the bottom of the screen.

Some people keep up-to-date statistics on the stock market, counting their spoils and regretting their losses. There is only one loss I regret; my ticker tapes keep me in a constant state of grief for you and all your boys; those you knew and those who didn't have the privilege.

An eighteen-year-old, baby-faced boy was killed yesterday. Fresh out of high school, two months in Iraq and now his body is coming home to Bradenton, Florida with the American flag draped over his casket.

Paul, I have such mixed feelings about this war now; not because you were taken from us, that was your destiny directed by your Father in heaven. We captured Saddam, our main objective, and we are trying to help these people achieve peace and democracy and all they want is for us to leave Iraq. The killing continues on both sides. I fear this war will come once more to our own country, as the resistance continues to grow.

I felt so much safer when I knew you were here.

June, 2004

We went to Helen, Georgia up in the mountains for a week's vacation. I love it in the mountains, where the air seems cooler and fresher. It was time for a break; I was ready to get out of the city and away from all the media that continues to hound us. I guess I just needed a rest from the world. Birgit and David are off to Germany to visit her family and when I return to Florida I will paint David's bedroom and put some graphics on the wall to surprise him when he returns.

Jessica opted to join us and I'm so glad she did; we don't get to spend much time with her now that she has a boyfriend. I know she will miss him but I will enjoy her visit so much. How I do relish these unexpected treats with her.

Lisa, Greyson and Olivia Rae joined us for a few days and I had so much fun being with them. In spite of Dad still being pretty sick he took Greyson down to the river behind our cabin and did some fishing with him. Jessie, Lisa and I did our share of shopping in town.

Are you ready for this one, Paul? While in town, I found a tattoo parlor; I had been looking for an artist that could do very fine lines, as I wanted to get my first—and maybe my last—tattoo. It is so beautiful and I'm glad I did it. Paul, I did it to honor you. I had found a picture on the Internet and would settle for nothing less. It's an American eagle's head with the American flag reflected on its face.

Above the eagle is written one single word: FREEDOM. Under the eagle is spelled your name. I know you think I'm out of my mind but then you always knew I was a strange one, didn't you?

Losing you has found me in a perpetual "what if" state of mind. Things that used to matter so much don't and other things I never paid attention to before mean the world to me. Like this tattoo.

I had talked about getting a tattoo forever but I guess I never found one that meant anything to me until right now. So far, reactions have been mixed. David and I would always buy those tattoos that you stick on so when I got back to the cabin and showed Dad he said, "It's not real; it will wash off in the shower." (Boy, was he in for a surprise!) After my shower poor Dad couldn't believe his eyes when it was still there. You know Dad; he just shook his head.

It's kinda strange how all the women in your life got a tattoo after your death to honor you. Birgit has a red heart on her left upper arm that says across the top (what else), "You're still the one" while inside the heart is your name. Your sister Lisa has a beautiful eagle in black on her left shoulder. The eagle looks like it is ready to attack; it's actually quite cool. Baby sister Cris has a pair of angel wings on her ankle, and now mine.

Do you think you had such a powerful effect on the women in your life?

The day after returning home I started to get busy with David's room. I painted it an off-white and found the perfect trim in a border of colorful large motorcycles in the background which kind of faded into the paper, much the same way as the eagle that is in my tattoo does.

David wanted an American flag painted on one wall so I did that, adding gold stars painted around the light switches and scattered around the room. Then the room was put back together and ready for his return. The day he returned I was there to see his expression; he couldn't have been happier with it. As I was leaving, David put his arms around me and so sweetly he said, "Thanks grandma, for my bedroom."

The moment he said that I saw the tender side of you.

Another honor for you, Paul: we got word yesterday that the post office here in Holiday will be renamed for you. Another day of pomp and ceremony, another reminder of your passing, another day we will smile and say, "Yes, we are so proud of him."

I know you are up there sitting on a cloud looking down on all of these honors that are being bestowed on you, and I'm sure you are telling your brothers up there that this is "...all insane, you were just doing your job."

I'll bet as you are saying that, you are just glad you don't have to be at all of them.

September 24, 2004

Today would have been your thirty-fourth birthday. I stayed in bed a long time today. I just didn't want to think about you or remember birthdays past. Finally I did make it out of bed and decided to stay so busy that I wouldn't have time to think about you. My mind must be controlled by my heart because that is not the way the day played out.

Are you surprised?

Often I would find myself drifting off in memories of you. All of a sudden I'd be dusting or opening the mail and your angelic face would appear and I could hear your laughter. I heard the laugh that sounded like a song to me; the one that told me you were into mischief. Your bright twinkling eyes and your smile. How could anyone forget you? I thought of the crazy stunts you would play on your little sister, like locking her in the rabbit cage just for the "fun" of it.

I remembered every broken bone you ever had and I laughed at the memory of seeing you after your brother and his friend had pushed you into a vat of cold tar, what a mess that was as the emergency room nurses tried to remove it from your delicate skin. Even now when I hear outrageous stories about you, I laugh and say, "Yep, that sounds like my boy."

I remembered how no matter what stunt you were pulling—or that was being pulled on you—you always had a quiet and easy way about you. You always had to have the last word, even if it was under your breath. Paul, I still heard you. Even then you had an air about you, you never went quietly, and you never raised your voice, yet you seemed to be the thunder in my ears.

Today was not a busy day, only in my mind.

October 15, 2004
Today is My Birthday

I didn't feel much like doing anything so I decided to go through some of my old poetry and stories I had written over the years for you kids. I came across a small book I had written several years ago that I wanted to give to all you kids as a gift of love. Amazingly, its title is, *If I Had Only Known*.

After reading it I sat and cried a long time over my procrastination. The book is about how little time we really have with our children. Now that I will never be able to give this book to you it has taken on a much deeper meaning. At that split second I made the decision to copy the pages, put them in a folder and give them to your siblings. Was that you whispering in my ear?

"Go on Mom," I could hear you say, "just do it."

October 29, 2004
The Post Office is Being Dedicated to You Today

The post office in Holiday was renamed in your honor today, and of course the ceremony was lovely. Paul, it was a warm sunny day, a day just like you would have loved to have been out in the gulf with Dad fishing, your favorite past time.

Lenny Dimick, the AMVETS chaplain, gave the invocation with tears in his eyes most of the time; he feels such a connection to you. The honorable congressman Mike Bilirakis did the dedication and plaque unveiling and was one of the guest speakers. Command Sgt. Major William Grant also was a speaker and gave a powerful and eloquent speech; he sounded more like a Southern preacher then a major.

Then one of your boys, Matthew Keller, took to the podium. Paul, he is so small in stature but so large in love. He spoke about what a great warrior you were and how much he respected you. Even if he hadn't said a word the reverence he felt for you would have shone through in his large, expressive eyes.

Some of your other boys were here for the dedication. Once again, they were sad but after the ceremony and back at the house they did loosen up and we all enjoyed each other's company after a time. They will be going back to Iraq soon and I could see the apprehension in their eyes.

SFC Paul R. Smith
Dedication Ceremony

Friday, October 29, 2004

Holiday Post Office
4737 Mile Stretch Drive
Holiday Fl 34690-9998

THE FLAG
OF THE
UNITED STATES
OF AMERICA

This is to certify that the accompanying flag was flown
over the United States Capitol at the request of the
Honorable Michael Bilirakis, Member of Congress.

Presented to Donald and Janice Pvirre
To commemorate the building dedication ceremony, October 29, 2004
Sergeant First Class Paul Ray Smith Post Office

"I'm prepared to give all that I am to ensure that all my boys make it home"

Sgt. 1st Class Paul Ray Smith

2004-056434-034

Alan M. Hantman, FAIA
Architect of the Capitol

December 8, 2004

I did it, Paul. Today I finished the book, *If I Had Only Known.* I finally put it all together in folders and gave it to Tony and Lisa. Then I gave your copy to Birgit. I know that you always knew how much I loved you, so I really wasn't sad to give the book to Birgit.

Lisa got it right away; she knew that the whole book said that you never have enough time to spend with your children before they are grown and gone. I hope it helps slow her pace a little and to remember to pay attention to everything her own children say to her. I have not heard from Tony or Birgit so I don't know if they even read it yet.

I have to tell you that the feeling I got from finishing and giving the little book was so gratifying. I guess I have you to thank for showing me how much I lost by waiting so long to put in the last few finishing touches. I paid the highest price for my procrastination; I just pray your sisters and brother learn from my mistake.

The family rode in the Veterans Day parade over in Temple Tarrace; once again you were honored and we continued to smile and wave. It was nice but it sure doesn't bring you home. I'm so tired, Paul. I don't mind telling you that I really don't want to do anymore of this.

It will soon be Christmas again; our second one without you. I know you are safe and watching over us but I can't help but be sad, even though I try not to be; it's really hard. I try to remember the funny things about you from Christmases past and, once I start, I find that I can't stop. What I recall is enough to fill a book.

You always loved what you got, even if you really didn't. No matter what you felt on the inside, you never let me know. Like that damn fruit cake I had been sending you every place you were stationed for Christmas because you said you "liked it," so I just kept sending them. You really should have told me you thought they were awful, but that just wasn't your way, was it Paul? I will buy one this year for you. No one will eat it but that's okay because we will all laugh and then I will throw it away after Christmas.

It will hurt too much to keep it around…

Another holiday memory quickly came to mind: The year we went out to church and then just rode around to see the lights and displays and, when we returned home and entered the house, there were Santa's gift to you kids under the tree.

That was the year that you and your little sister were absolutely sure that there really *was* a Santa. Well, how else could the gifts have gotten there? The confusion and amazement on your face was my Christmas gift that year, Paul. I have wonderful Christmas pictures of you—they will have to be my comfort this year.

We are going to be with Lisa and Brad this year, as Birgit and David are going to spend the holidays with her friend Tonja in Heinsville.

I will miss you so much again this year. I love you, son.

Please tell me you know that by now...

14

Another New Year Without You

✦

January, 2005

Christmas has passed and the New Year has begun. Sometimes it's hard to fathom that it's actually been twenty-one months since you died; it seems like just yesterday. Rumors are swirling that you are, in fact, going to get the Medal-of-Honor, but we have not officially heard that yet.

The guest book on your web site continues to get comments. Every time I go on the site and read the messages that people have written, I am truly over-whelmed by the depths of their touching sentiments. People from all over the country and even beyond our borders have written to express their gratitude, their pride, their honesty. Their outpouring of emotion is all too familiar to me; it's what I'm doing in this journal. I am so amazed at the love that is out there for you and the appreciation they have for your sacrifice so that they may live free.

Well kiddo, for a young man that never wanted recognition for anything good he did, what do you think now? Knowing you like I do, I know you are saying, "I'm really glad I'm not there."

Even if you don't get the medal, son, you will never be forgotten for your commitment to duty; your family will be sure to pass your story on for as long as we live.

You are still *my* hero.

January 15, 2005

As I sit here and think back over the last 21 months it is still so hard to believe you are dead and not coming home. I keep saying this but it is a fact; for me it still seems so surreal. I continue to watch CNN and the news of the war because "your boys" are still there and I worry about them and pray for their safety and safe return home.

Soon...

For all this time, 21 months, I have been so angry, so sad. I stay depressed most of the time. I continue to ask myself, "Why? Why you? Why this war?" I have so many other questions that, like these, I'm sure will never be answered. When I ask the Lord, He tells me to "be still and listen."

I wake up every morning and have to remind myself of the truth; the truth that I hate. I stay angry at President Bush for starting this war. I know he didn't start it but I need to blame someone. Why not start at the top? I'm even angry with God, God forgive me, but He could have saved you. So why didn't He? Can you believe I'm even angry with *you*, Paul? I'm angry with you for not giving that job that took your life to someone else.

I don't want to be angry anymore, Paul, but I don't quite know how *not* to be.

15

Liberation

✦

January 30, 2005

January 30th. Twenty-one months after your death. Believe it or not, today I am not angry, only fifteen days after saying I didn't know how *not* to be. As I watched the brave Iraqi people walk for miles today to cast their votes under threatening circumstances, a vote for democracy in their country for the fist time in three decades, I cried and was so happy for them, but at the same time so sad for my own loss.

I watched the faces of those people—some looked so happy, some looked scared to death—but they were all willing to risk their lives to leave the safety of their homes to show the world what they really wanted for themselves: freedom.

I cried most of the day as I heard of the deaths of some of those that were killed on the march for freedom. I cried for the ones who died this day and continue to ask myself why so many people in this world are against freedom. I just don't get it, Paul. I don't understand what war is all about.

I wish you were here to tell me.

February 1, 2005

Captain Smith, now Colonel Smith, of the Pentagon called Birgit today to say that your nomination for the medal has been signed by one person and all it needs now is the President's signature and it will be so. Well Paul, are you still saying, "It's no big deal, I was only doing my job?"

Boy, do I have mixed feelings about all this. I am so humbled and honored that you will never be forgotten for what you did. I know you say it's "no big deal" but, honey, for every mother that welcomes her soldier home from the war, what you did is a *very* big deal indeed.

I wish I could be one of those mothers, but at the same time I am happy for them. It's also a big deal for the Iraqi people; those people that you wanted to help free are now voting—under much protest by some and loss of life to others—but they are earning freedom one day at a time. It was a very big deal, Paul. You always made a difference in everything you did and so we were not surprised by your actions, only sad that you are not one of the soldiers coming home.

The lessons you taught all of us will never be forgotten. Your kindness that never went unnoticed, the way everything had to be done right or not at all, everything about you is a treasure that you will now get to share with the world through this marvelous opportunity to be remembered.

Most of all, Paul, it was your love that we all will remember—and miss—the most. I don't believe I will ever meet another person with all your fine qualities; we were all so lucky to have known you. What can I say except I'm so proud of you, but then, you always *were* my hero. I love you so, and I will miss you till the day I cross over and I meet you once again, God willing.

Same Day
Evening

Funny how our mind congers up images just when we seem to need them the most. I was outside looking up at the stars tonight; looking for you and, like a video running past my eyes, I *saw* you. I know that when we die and go to heaven just like here on earth, we are in service to our Lord. I saw you, my horrible fisherman.

I saw you on the ark and you were bringing in a very large fish; you looked at me with that very special smile that told me you are fine and are now fishing for the Lord, only now you really are catching "the big ones." Your faithfulness has earned you the rightful spot as head fisherman for the Lord's table and once again, if only for a moment, I am happy.

February 2, 2005

Today the President addressed the nation and I watched, hanging on every word he said. I absorbed the very atmosphere of that room. I watched as President Bush introduced a woman from Iraq whose father had been killed by Saddam. As she stood shaking with nerves and tears in her eyes, as she raised her ink stained finger I was overwhelmed with the knowledge that you, my son, my hero had helped to make this possible.

Then a mother who had also lost her son in the desert bent down to embrace this woman from Iraq. At that very moment I was so proud to be an American, at that moment in time I knew that your death was not in vain.

At last, what you believed in was coming true...

16

It Is Happening

◆

March 22, 2005

It is official; you *will* **receive the** Medal-of-Honor. Once again, my feelings are very mixed. A part of me is filled with extreme pride for what you've done. At the same time, though, I can't help but be a little mad at you.

After all, where do you think you got your desire for privacy?

Now your whole family has been thrust into the limelight; a light we would just assume not have shone on us. The media will want to know every little detail about who you are. I just want to keep what we had private. I want to protect you from the world. I sound crazy, I suppose, like a mother lion trying to protect her little cub. Now there will be no privacy.

All I want is for my memories to be my own, but I know that the world will want to know you personally; they will want to know this man who loved his freedom—and his country—so much that he would lay down his life for it.

March 24th

Interviews with the Army. Major Leela Dawson from McDill Air Force Base is Birgit's liaison officer for the press. We met her today and she is a very personable woman who seems to be very caring.

It is starting to get quite nuts since we got the news that you will be awarded the medal. Today we gave interviews for the Army; we met at Birgit's, not sure what to expect. Major Dawson, the interviewer, and the photographer were all there; they asked all the right questions, they took a lot of pictures and again we relived the sadness that we are all living through; our own personal war, the battle we fight every day.

Tony was so proud and thoughtful in the things that he said; you would have been very proud of your brother, too. I could tell by the things he said that he misses you and I could feel that inside of him; he wishes that the two of you would have been much closer. Your time with him was so short. I know if you had stayed around home longer instead of joining the Army the two of you would have gotten close.

I just hope he holds tight to all the wonderful times that the two of you *did* have together, and puts any regrets aside. Regrets are such a waste of time. I know that now. After all, I have filled dozens or more suitcases with regrets. Not until I gave them to the Lord did I learn that old luggage is too heavy and too much a waste of valuable life and time.

Tomorrow is David's eleventh birthday; he wants to spend the night so I will do some fun things with him. On my way home I will order the birthday cake he saw at the grocery store a few weeks ago while we were shopping. True to form, he made sure I knew that the one with the motorcycles on it was the one he wanted.

He's getting to be more like you every day…

March 25, 2005
David's 11th Birthday

8:30 A.M. and my birthday boy woke up to hugs and kisses and a very off-key rendition of Happy Birthday.

Dad called from work to wish him a Happy Birthday and so did Lisa. He said he was glad that someone besides grandpa and me remembered his birthday.

We started our day with a little clean up of the front walkway and driveway. I asked him to sweep the walk and he promptly told me he "didn't know how to use a broom." I know you must have been laughing because he was right; he really *didn't* know how to use a broom. It didn't make any difference to me; I showed him how to use one just the same. (How's *that* for a birthday present?)

I remember you using that same statement with me on more than one occasion. He is so much like you in so many ways but he really is quite lazy, which was so *unlike* you at this age. To "cure" him I try very hard to have him help me with my chores when he comes over; we do things together and he seems to like doing them with me, but for some reason he just hates doing the chores alone. I don't mind helping him; it keeps us close.

We started with a movie, his choice. He wanted to see *Robots*, and so it was; this was his day. It was okay; I think we had more fun just being together. Soon we were going to the place he really was waiting for: Stop and Play. He knew it was a place similar to Chuck E. Cheese but had never been there before. When we got there he saw everything that was there and promptly informed me that it was ten times *better* then Chuck E. Cheese. We got twenty dollars worth of tokens and he went to town. You talk about a lucky little guy; he says he got it from you, and I believed him.

We went to pick up Jessica so she could come over to the house and have dinner with us and spend time with David. I think it was a treat for us all; now that she is out on her own we don't get to spend a lot of time with her.

When I had asked David what he wanted for his birthday dinner it was as if you had answered. He wanted Grandpa to cook him a "delicious steak on the grill." Your Dad was more then happy to oblige.

When we got home Dad had already picked up the cake as planned with three Happy Birthday balloons. He was setting out David's presents and getting ready to start the grill. You could tell by David's face he was so happy that we hadn't forgotten a thing. Just before he left to go home he took one of his balloons outside. He said he wanted to "set it free." As he looked into the sky he said that this balloon was for you. He misses you so much in so many ways, but he still doesn't talk about you.

So, Paul, did you like your balloon?

March 27, 2005

We have received word that you will be awarded the Medal-of-Honor on April 4th of this year, just two weeks from today. The ceremony will be held on the anniversary of your death; how fitting. Again, mixed feelings fill my soul; my heart can't seem to mend. I guess it will never mend but the scabs are opening wide again, and the tears seem to be pouring from my eyes like buckets of rain at any given time. We will be leaving for Washington on April 3, 2005. I hope I will be able to control this flood that seems to come without warning.

I will try to be strong for you, Paul.

I am trying to keep this whole thing in perspective and it is so hard for me. I just want to wake up in the morning and not have the main focus of every day be on your death and the brave act that has you getting the medal in the first place. Keeping this in perspective is hard; I just want to be private and now the world will want to know all about you and your life. Knowing how private you always were I almost feel like I am betraying you. Keeping this in perspective, I know that in David's lifetime this all will be very important to him. In my lifetime, I just want to be private, too, and remember that you were always my hero.

Is that so much to ask?

17

The Final Chapter

◆

April 17, 2005

We have been back from Washington for seven days now and I am still trying to digest and sort out the three days we spent in the nation's capital.

Our escort, SFC Vernon Pollard, was all military, very tall and handsome; just like you. Every part of him was spit shined, just as you would have demanded. In fact, in many ways his demeanor kind of reminded me of you; all military business. At exactly 9:30 a.m. a large blue army van from Mc Dill Air Force Base picked us up and we were off to the airport to catch our plane to Washington, DC.

Most of the family sat close to the front of the plane so our ride was rather smooth considering that there was some turbulence. About thirty minuets into the flight the Captain came on the speaker to inform the whole plane that the family of the Medal-of-Honor recipient was on the plane and on the way to Washington, DC to accept the medal on Monday. It was very nice of him but it was also embarrassing; we are all very proud of you but, just like you, hate to have the attention drawn to us. I have to remember that the nation needs this type of celebration; with so much going wrong in the world your medal can be a shining point in this ongoing war.

We arrived in Washington right on time and were whisked off to our hotel, the Washington Hilton. It was very nice, Paul, a real five-star affair; nothing but the best. Shortly after arriving we had a meeting with Vernon, our escort, so he could give us the three-day itinerary.

For today, Sunday evening, there was to be a sit down dinner for family, VIPs, and invited guests. The food was outstanding; you would have loved being there, among family and friends; there was lots of laughter, just like our own family get togethers. Your laughter was missed tonight, though. We were able to catch up with friends we hadn't seen for a while, and we all talked about you and how we all were doing and getting on. Some were doing well, others were just doing.

I still don't know in which category I belonged…

Monday; April 4, 2005
The White House

Those that were able to sleep had to get up early for breakfast as our bus to the White House was to leave at eight sharp. Of course, being on military time they really meant eight sharp! We all gathered in the foyer of the hotel, and everyone was so dressed up in their Sunday best; you would have thought that we were going to meet the President or something like that. Jokes like that one kept me going. I had to keep thinking on funny things or light issues, otherwise I was afraid that I would break down and my soft, naked underbelly would be in full view. I had to be strong for you, for your family, but I didn't *feel* strong.

I felt more like crawling under a rock till this was all over.

Dad and I boarded the bus that was waiting for us before the others and as I watched the rest of the family coming toward us, I had such a peaceful and proud feeling pass through me. Paul, I truly have been blessed. First came Birgit, Jessica, and my sweet David.

In his black suit with blue shirt, David looked so much like you did at his age. He looked relaxed and thoughtful; I wish I could have read his mind right about then. He could have taught me something about grace under pressure. He acted excited about going to the White House. Then came Lisa, Brad, Greyson and that little princess, Olivia Rae.

Lisa, in her tailored blue suit with dainty little white pearls around her neck, looked for all the world like a movie star. She is so beautiful, a very classy woman and an awesome mother. Bradley, looking so proud of his family, was a striking figure himself. He is such a wonderful man; he had so much respect for you, Paul, and now the sadness that we all are wearing today shows on his face.

In his sport coat and sweater, Greyson looked so Ivy League; he is a carbon copy of his Daddy, which is a good thing; such a handsome little man. Little Rae looked just like Mommy did at that age in her ever so soft mint green dress with satin ribbons.

Paul, these are pictures of my family—of *your* family—that will be forever engraved on my heart. (Were you watching? Silly question; I know you were!) Your brother, Tony, and Janee were the next to board the bus. As I watched Tony looking so very much in control, I saw behind his eyes to the extreme sadness that he carries with him and, once again, I wish I could make the pain go away. He is such a handsome man and I feel that with your passing he and I are a little bit closer.

Another painful lesson for your family???

The President and Mrs. Bush
request the pleasure of your company
at a ceremony and reception to be held at
The White House
on Monday, April 4, 2005
at three o'clock

On the occasion of

the presentation of the

Medal of Honor

(Posthumously)

to

SFC Paul R. Smith, USA

THE PRESIDENT

welcomes you to

THE WHITE HOUSE

on the occasion of the presentation of the

MEDAL OF HONOR
(POSTHUMOUSLY)

to

SERGEANT FIRST CLASS
PAUL R. SMITH
UNITED STATES ARMY

Monday, April 4, 2005

Arriving at the White House, all security measures were taken as we entered into the east lobby and down a hall that had at least twenty-five feet (or more) ceilings. As one might expect, the decor was nothing but the best: Italian marble floors, brass as far as the eye could see, not a single detail had been overlooked. Historical pictures, busts of past presidents, and portraits of former first lades adorned every hall we walked through. To say that being in this magnificent building made me feel small and insignificant would be the understatement of the year.

As we stopped at a spot just before a large staircase to our right, we were asked if anyone needed to use "the facilities." There were two doors, one on the left for the women and across the hall one for the men. Of course, everyone wanted to see the bathrooms so we were allotted time to visit them and take pictures.

The ladies room was decorated in rich, soft colors with a large, round table in the center of the room that had a vase with flowers that matched the room—the bouquet itself was almost three feet high! Beautiful pictures and flowers prevailed and the windows were almost as high as the ceiling. In the lavatory itself, there were more flowers and highly-polished brass.

I was such a bad girl in there, Paul: I stole a hand towel from the washroom! Of the White House!!! In my mind it really wasn't stealing, though. After all, they were made out of paper, kind of like a paper towel, but very soft, feeling almost like cloth. These towels had the President's seal on them in gold. I'm sure they were designed for the very purpose of becoming a souvenir for some lucky visitor and put there for a person just like me. (At least, that's what I told myself!)

As we left the room I was glad to see that almost every lady had one of the souvenirs with them. I can't even begin to tell you about the flowers, Paul. They blossomed in every color of the rainbow and in every species that I have ever seen—and some I hadn't. Every room had very large arrangements, all with colors specifically designed to match that room and its decor.

The very sight of them took your breath away; at one point the smell reminded me of your funeral and I had to excuse myself while I tried to hold back tears that seemed to be ready to flow at any time now. As you might expect, everyone was very understanding; I think because, like me, they too were like dams about ready to burst.

We climbed the stairs to our right and found ourselves in a large foyer, once again with windows that matched the heights of the ceilings. Those windows looked out over very precise, manicured gardens. As we passed through the foyer a military band was playing music to our left and as I looked above them, I saw a staircase with red carpets and large chandeliers. (Later I was told that this was the staircase to the President's White House residence.)

Our escorts delivered the family and VIPs into the green room in the east wing of the White House. I'll bet you will never guess why it is called the green room; you got it: green it was. This shade of green was one I had never seen before, though, or did I just think that because it looked so much richer with all the gold in the drapes that fell from the ceiling and adorned the large fireplace mantel. Why, there was even gold in the wallpaper.

Yes, it was very fancy and very lovely, especially the view of the gardens from these windows and the lush lawns that seemed to go on forever. In this room we mixed and mingled with very important dignitaries and past recipients of the Medal-of-Honor. I was very impressed with them and wanted to talk to them some more, but with all that was going on my mind was not in a place that allowed me to just relax and enjoy the company of such great men. My feelings were being pushed to the limit as I thought about you not being among them and in this room with us.

Birgit and the children were soon escorted to another room were they would meet with President Bush for a short time before the ceremonies were to begin. I wish I could have been a fly on the wall, but Birgit said that they really didn't do that much talking. I still have not asked David what the President said to him but maybe he would rather keep that to himself. For now, anyway. Like much of our trip, there are treasures yet to be discovered by us all. One day we will have to have a reenactment just to sit around and visit and swap stories.

While they were gone the rest of the party was brought into the room adjacent to the green room. Now we were in the blue room, and it was the same scenario as before: very royal blue and sumptuous with golds of all hues and richness. This is the same room we were brought back to after the medal had been awarded. But while there this time we mixed and mingled as before and more pictures were taken.

Then we were told that the President, Birgit and the kids were on the way in, so we all lined up to be introduced to the President before going into the east room for the presentation. Then entered the President, Birgit, David and Jessie. Birgit went down the line and introduced the President to the whole family as we stood in line, mouths agape.

He was a bit shorter then I expected, although I thought he was much better looking in person than when I saw him on television or the few times I saw him in person at rallies. Then again, perhaps this occasion had softened his looks.

When he was introduced to me and he took my hand there was a calming of my spirit; the sincere look in his eyes made me feel easy and comfortable for the first time that day. I thought that he would intimidate me but, in reality, the feeling was quite the opposite. He thanked me for raising such a great man.

Like you, Paul, it was hard for me to take credit—or a complement—so I simply said that it was mostly the Lord's work. How simple can you get? But I so believe this statement is the truth; then again, I must have had a bigger influence on you than even I have considered. Just yesterday Dad said that you had gotten a lot of your traits from me; it made me cry.

I felt so privileged to be in the White House and in Washington, DC to be a part of the honors that were being bestowed on you, but once again my heart was breaking all over. For a while there I could get up in the morning and breathe, but today I feel as if it were yesterday that we heard of your death. The pain and awareness is so very acute today.

Your family and friends were escorted down the red carpeted hall to the east room, were the ceremonies would take place. All along the hall were the media and other invited guests. It seemed like it took us an eternity to reach the room, which in reality couldn't have been more than one hundred yards away. This room is where your son David would accept the medal for you. We were all shown to our seats in the front row and soon the President was announced and walked to the stage.

He was joined by Chaplain Hicks to deliver the invocation. The President's speech was nothing but true and heartfelt by all. President Bush quoted a part of the letter you wrote home to Dad and I before you had been killed. He said that you wrote, "I am willing to give all that I am so that my boys would return home." He said that "on this day two years ago, Sergeant Smith gave his all for his men."

"Five days later Baghdad fell," he went on to say, "and today, we bestow upon Sergeant Smith the first Medal of Honor in the war on terror. He's also the first to be awarded this new Medal of Honor flag, authorized by the United States Congress." He said "...we count ourselves blessed to have soldiers like you who put their lives on the line to advance the cause of freedom and protect the American people."

He said you were "a boy transformed into a man and leader." He made us all laugh when he said that due to some of your pursuits you occasionally earned what the Army calls "extra duty"—scrubbing floors. He went on to say that one of the great changes in your life came when you were shipped off to Saudi Arabia to fight in the first Gulf War. How very true this was.

He said that "...there as a young combat engineer you learned that your training had a purpose and could save lives on the battlefield." He said "...that when you returned from that war you were determined that other soldiers would benefit from the lessons that you learned." He went on to say, "...that you earned your sergeant's stripes and became known as a stickler for detail." He said that your seriousness wasn't always appreciated by the greener troops under your direction. "Those greener troops oftentimes found themselves to do tasks over and over again, until they got it right."

Specialist Michael Seaman, one of your boys, who is with us today, says, "He, (meaning you) was hard in training because he knew we had to be hard in battle. Specialist Seaman will also tell you that he and others are alive today because of Sergeant Smith's discipline..."

Then President Bush went on to describe your actions on that fateful day, how you manned a .50 caliber machine-gun defending your troops in the compound near the Baghdad Airport. As he spoke, I was once again in that courtyard with you and all the healing I had done in the two years was suddenly gone; I felt like it was yesterday. He continued by saying that your actions that day saved more than 100 American soldiers.

"Like every one of the men and women in uniform who have served in Operation Iraqi Freedom, Sergeant Paul Smith was a volunteer. We thank his family for the father, husband, son and brother who can never be replaced," said the President. He concluded by thanking the living Medal of Honor recipients who attended the ceremony: John Baker, Barney Barnum, Bernie Fisher, Al Rascon and Brian Thacher.

Then the beautiful Medal of Honor flag was presented for the first time. It is light blue with gold fringe on three sides bearing thirteen white stars in the same configuration as on the Medal of Honor itself. I was told that the flag commemorates the sacrifice and blood shed for our freedoms and gives emphasis to the Medal of Honor being the highest award for valor by an individual serving in the Armed Forces of the United States.

As I looked over at the living recipients I couldn't help but picture you seated there with them and I could see your beautiful eyes reflecting the royal blue from the ribbon. Why were they saved and not you? Sadly, it was just another question that will never be answered. The President then asked for the citation to be read by a military aide and we once again heard the story retold. Then Birgit, Jessica and David walked to the stage to join President Bush.

As I watched David standing next to the President, getting ready to accept the medal, I thought to myself, "He is standing so tall and brave." Paul, it reminded me so much of you. Always composed, almost standing at attention, in the moment that need be, but so wonderfully free and happy when not needing to be.

He is such a handsome little guy and so much the song in my heart. I must thank you, Paul, for this gift of yourself. When David was first handed the wooden box that held the medal he had a strange, sad, sideways smile on his face. I wish I knew what he was thinking just then. Maybe he was thinking the same thing I was at that precise moment: this is no consolation.

As I looked at the medal and the bright ribbon from which it hung I couldn't help but see it around your neck, the blue ribbon reflecting in your eyes; making them blue for the day. As I gazed over at the living recipients I felt so cheated that you were not among them; it just wasn't meant to be.

Little did I realize that we had to walk that same red carpeted hallway back to the opposite end to enter the State Dining Room for a reception and refreshments. Now the media and their prying, flashing cameras were in every available space. Suddenly, Birgit, Lisa and I were whisked away to an outside garden to give an interview.

As we passed along the hall back to the dining room the band was playing music and I just wanted to stop the world, linger and listen. The brunch in the State Dining room was a pure sugar high. David, Geyson and Olivia Rae were in heaven with the sweet treats and once again David was a free butterfly and being a little boy. While I was outside giving an interview I guess I missed the highlight of the brunch when sister-in-law Barbara danced with Vernon, the escort, in the foyer! (I would have given anything to see that.)

With the interviews over and the President returning to his routine schedule, the day was finally at an end and we returned to the hotel to have a free evening to do what we wanted.

I didn't want to think about this day anymore so my sister, Sharon, her husband, Robert, and Janee were going to take me on a bus tour of the city. Just the thing to keep my mind off the day. We all met in the lobby of the hotel at the prescribed time and waited. And waited. And then we waited some more. The bus was forty five-minutes late and in that short time span my total supply of energy was drained right out of me; Dad and I declined the tour and went back to our room.

The day had taken more of a toll on me than I realized. My mind was still going in circles trying to digest the day's activities; the anticipation of the next day, never thinking it could have been any harder then today was.

Sleep came slowly; the morning came too fast…

Tuesday
April 5, 2005

Today was going to be very long for all of us and I could already see the strain on the faces of my family and friends as we departed the hotel at nine a.m. sharp. First stop, the Pentagon.

Once again we were all dressed in our finery as we took a bus to the Pentagon. We first had a tour of the Pentagon, going down back halls and secret passageways that I'm sure the every day tour people never saw. At least, we didn't see any other tours going on while we were there.

As our tour proceeded down hallways lined with historic pictures our knowledgeable tour guide explained each one. It was amazing, Paul; I learned more history in this one day than I did in all fourteen years of school. We entered into a general or common area that surprised most of us. This area had eateries and shops of all kinds; it looked like a mall in the middle of the Pentagon underground. This stop seemed to sum up our tour in general: happy and informative.

As we traveled along the hallways you could see the extreme security around every corner. The heavy security measures were both reassuring and unsettling at the same time. Then our tour came upon the very spot where the plane crashed into the Pentagon on 9-11.

Standing in the hall our tour guide told us that on the outside of the wall was one of the original blocks from that day. According to our guide, it had been put back all charred and mangled to stand as a reminder (as if anyone would need a reminder).

Off of this hall there was a tiny little room inside an archway. As we all stood inside this tiny room the atmosphere was suddenly that of being in a church. The light was dim, the walls a shiny silver. At one end of the room was a large black marble slab that said, "September 11, 2001: The Lost and Missing," and beneath this were the names of 184 people lost and missing from inside the Pentagon and on American Airlines Flight 77 on that day; all etched in gold. I don't mind telling you, Paul, it sent chills through my soul.

At the opposite end of the room was another black marble slab that read, "The Purple Heart Medal," and under this the real medal was on display. Against the wall that ran the length of the room there was a table with a guest book on it, so we all wrote our names in it and some wrote a message.

We all left the Pentagon Memorial with sadness and awe and in silence as we continued on our tour. As we traveled further into the bowls of the Pentagon back halls you knew that no tour was taken back here. Our tour came to a "T" in the hallway and there in the middle was a very large poster on a tripod that took my breath away. The poster was in different shades of blue.

Sergeant First Class Paul R. Smith
MEDAL OF HONOR
WAR ON TERRORISM

In the background was your picture, Paul, in full Army gear and your special smile beaming out at me; there was also the group picture of your unit that had been taken in the desert behind you. The lower half of the picture had the Medal-of-Honor stretched across the poster. The beautiful medal that hangs from the silken ribbon has a small plaque with one word on it and being held in the talons of a gold eagle: "VALOR." The family was given 8 x 12 posters of the image to take home, mine is over my computer next to the picture of you graduating from Ft. Leonard Wood and the very small urn that holds some of your ashes.

I look at it every day.

We were now in the inner sanctum of the Pentagon, the hallways were smaller but the importance of these offices were marked with brass nameplates. As we entered into an office that appeared to be a conference room we waited quietly, most of us still in awe of the access to which we'd been granted in your name. While there we met with the Chief of Staff, General Schoomaker, and Sergeant Major of the Army, Kenneth Preston.

At the time I didn't know that we were to have coffee with them, as well as with the Secretary of the Army, the Honorable Francis J. Harvey. Soon a door that linked this room with another opened and we were escorted into Dr. Harvey's private office. There was a round table off to the side set with fine china and dainty little pastries.

As Dr. Harvey greeted us I couldn't help but think what a charming man he was. I wish I hadn't been so nervous, Paul. I would have liked to talk to him at length. At the time I was not aware of the fact that he had gone to college at Notre Dame. I later learned that was the university in South Bend, Indiana; I had been born in the little sister city of Misawalka, Indiana. That would have at least given me something to say. As it was, I felt so out of my league.

The coffee was served and oh so welcomed; we'd only had one cup at breakfast and we were all *way* overdue for another! As we had our coffee, the Honorable Harvey, General Schoomaker and Sergeant Major Preston presented Birgit, David, Jessica and myself with lovely wooden keepsake boxes with their names and the Department of the Army seal on it. I use my box to keep the many challenge coins and business cards I was given on our trip to Washington. We had wonderful pictures taken with all these wonderful men and soon it was time to move on.

Then our entire party moved down the hall to the Secretary of Defense, Donald Rumsfeld's office. There Mr. and Mrs. Rumsfeld were waiting for us and greeted us as if we had known them forever. Mrs. Rumsfeld seemed to have an acute sense of awareness about her and I enjoyed talking to this lovely lady. She seemed so unpretentious and down to earth. I know if I had met her at a social gathering she would have become a friend. She smiled easily, just like her husband, and I could tell that they made a beautiful couple.

Mr. Rumsfeld's office was huge; if I had to guess I would say the square footage had to be at least nine hundred, and what a wonderful office it was. As Dad and I walked around admiring the paintings and sculptures Mr. and Mrs. Rumsfeld took the time to talk to each one of us and express their deepest sympathies.

In the sitting area of his office David and I had been looking at a scrap of metal that was mounted on a polished piece of wood. Mr. Rumsfeld came over to tell us that it was a piece of the airplane that crashed into the Pentagon. He spoke softly as he recalled that fateful day and I could see the sadness on his face. On a round table with a glass top at one end of the room we gathered around while he told us that under the glass were two voting ballots that were used in the Iraqi Elections.

My eyes were glued to the ballots and I knew that it was partly due to what you did and believed in that these ballots had even been used and again. At that moment I thanked you in a silent prayer. I have a beautiful picture of the whole family with Mr. Rumsfeld taken in his office, but I so wish that Mrs. Rumsfeld had been in the picture as well.

Now, on to the Hall of Heroes
11:00 A.M.

Arriving at the Hall of Heroes was a short walk but outside of the hall there were closed circuit televisions on one wall and chairs set up for the overflow. Entering into the Hall of Heroes I was surprised that the room was not much bigger than it was but the only thing that really registered with me was the gigantic forms of the Medal of Honors that hung from the ceiling behind the small stage area.

The family was escorted to the front row and seated before the rest of the room filled up. Directly behind us were the rest of family, friends and invited guests. On the other side of the isle Mr. and Mrs. Rumsfeld, The Honorable Harvey, General Schoomaker and other dignitaries sat. Behind them were your boys, Paul, and many others in military dress. I was so happy that your boys were able to come back to the States for this award ceremony, as I know you would have wanted them there.

The National Anthem was sung and introductions were made and then Mr. Rumsfeld stepped to the podium. He started out by pointing out that the World Trade Center opened 32 years ago that very week. He said it was hard to understand "the evil that drove extremists to topple those towers and rip an ugly gash in the building (the Pentagon)."

He continued in a somber tone: "But this much we do know. From our earliest days, America has had the good fortune to be blessed by volunteers who have stepped forward to defend our citizens and our way of life," Rumsfeld said. "A few of them have famous names, some undertake crucial missions in secret, and others live in gracious anonymity. But each is driven, I believe, by love of country, a devotion to duty, and the hope of leaving their loved ones and future generations a safer world."

Then he turned to the family, welcomed us and said that we all, "Saw their boy become a man who crossed deserts to topple tyrants. And now Paul joins America's most admired fraternity—those awarded the Medal of Honor for service above and beyond the call of duty." He said, "It is a fraternity so revered that President Harry S. Truman once confided to a soldier he decorated: 'I'd rather have this Medal than be president.'"

Then Birgit, Jessica and David joined Mr. Harvey, Gen. Schoomaker and Mr. Rumsfeld on the podium for the unveiling of the picture and citation. Once again the citation was read and by now I think the family was numb as we sat there in a fog. Little David's face looked tired and frozen as he and Jessica stood, one on each side of the tripod where the plaque and citation rested. Then they dropped the black velvet cloth that covered it.

I was so surprised at the picture that the Army had used of you. I can tell you, Paul, it was not a very flattering one. It reminded me of when I saw you at your sister's wedding and you looked so very tired. Perhaps they thought its grittiness and realism made you look heroic, but I wished they'd consulted me first! Oh well, what's one picture? You will always be beautiful to me. I don't know what David was thinking as the cloth came off but I noticed that he never smiled once.

Then Birgit took the podium; she said how proud we all were to be accepting the medal in your name. She said, "Paul loved his country, he loved the Army, he loved his soldiers and he loved being a Sapper. He died doing what he loved. I'm grateful the Army gave Paul the opportunity to fulfill his dream of serving his country." Then she went on to say, "I would like to thank all of the soldiers who influenced Paul as he advanced through his military career. Most described him as tough, fair, and always putting the mission and his soldiers first."

Birgit continued, "Paul was proud of all of his troops, particularly those in 2nd Platoon, Bravo Company, 11th Engineers. He was dedicated to duty and unwilling to accept less than the best." She was so right about all of this. She described the military man you were to a "T."

She went on to say, "Because of this award, Paul's story of uncommon valor will forever be remembered." Then she encouraged others, "As soldiers, I encourage you to tell your stories, because the American people and the world will better understand the sacrifices of Paul, and others like him, one soldier's story at a time." How else could she end but by, "HOOAH and God bless." Every soldier in the room and those outside—and your family included—stood and repeated her, "HOOAH, HOOAH!"

As the children joined Birgit and the dignitaries back onstage I looked at all the oversized pieces of marble that hung on the walls in that room. I knew that each marble slab was from a different war and etched on each were the names of Medal of Honor recipients from that war.

At the end of one wall was a large marble slab that had a very long, very black cloth covering it. I knew it was for you so I didn't think I would have any more surprises. Once again David stood stone faced and looking tired as he and Jessie pulled the cloth off the marble. As the cloth fell to the floor revealing the marble plaque that read "War on Terrorism" I think I stopped breathing for a short while. I was so taken back by the sight of one name and one name only on this huge plaque—your name is the first and only name on it. Paul, once again the reality of your death was shoved in my face. Off to the right of the pink marble it read one word, "Iraq," and under it "Smith, Paul R. Sergeant First Class USA."

The realization of knowing that you are now forever in the history of our great and mighty nation and your name is carved in stone was somehow comforting. At the very least, it will never be forgotten and in a very small way I suppose that is a consolation for what you must have endured.

What I will endure for the rest of my life is no consolation; my only consolation is that my time here on earth is but a raindrop in the ocean compared to the eternity I will spend with you on the other side. For me, there will never be any consolation; nothing will ever bring you home, but I know that one day we will meet again.

It was a moment frozen in time even as I felt frozen to the chair I was sitting in. Once again many pictures were taken and the family walked to the podium to form a receiving line. I know we must have shook hands with every person in the Pentagon that day, or so it seemed. It seemed a small price to pay; in many ways I think the honor meant as much to them as it did to us.

Leaving the Pentagon and boarding our bus for the last leg of our journey to Arlington Cemetery, I couldn't help but think that our family would fight this war every day for the rest of our lives. En route to Arlington I saw the strain of the day taking its toll on the faces of my children. I knew the feeling; I couldn't wait for this day to be over so I could go back to the hotel and just try to breathe again.

I had seen Arlington National Cemetery on television many times so I didn't think it would be much of a surprise for me. As we entered the gates, however, it was as if I had never seen it before. My mind went back to wars that had been fought even before my time. The thought that every one of these perfectly straight white stones—it looked like a perfectly tended rock garden—represented a life lost for my freedom made me want to cry. I thought of the millions of tears that had watered the hills of this cemetery and the very breath in me was silent.

Being in this cemetery was like none other I had ever seen or been in before. I had not realized that Arlington was so large, and still the bus just kept passing those endless fields full of white headstones. I was so taken back by the sheer size of Arlington and the thought of all the tears that must have been shed on the lawns of these rolling hills for all that gave the ultimate sacrifice just like you did, Paul.

Once again I am almost speechless to think that an ordinary, skinny, funny little boy from the south side of Tampa is now among the most elite group of men and women that ever walked this earth. My ordinary boy who grew up to be an extraordinary man.

Front row, center stage, grave-side

Finally we arrive and are escorted past the guests, watching your boys standing at attention and looking very smart but very tired. The ever-present media is in one area and a military band is seated opposite where we are being seated. There is a headstone with a light blue cloth over it a little way up the hill. Paul, I know it is for you.

As I sit here listening and watching to the presentation of the colors, the national anthem, the invocation and remarks, my eyes are wandering up the hill to a soldier that is just standing there waiting. Is he a guard? What is he doing up there among the trees? He is far enough away that I couldn't tell.

As the music started to play my eyes moved back down the hill to the blue cloth and the little white flowers that were growing randomly everywhere among the many stones. As the music played a soldier walked up to the front and started to sing. His voice was strong and deep and by the first line of his song family, friends, invited guests and many of the media had started to cry.

As I looked over to where David sat I noticed that he was stone faced; not a single tear fell. I know that his heart must have been breaking with the words of the song. Once again, his feelings were hidden in that secret place that the two of you had. The name of the song was "Hero for a day."

Didn't they know, Paul, that you were the hero of my life, not just one day?

Sgt. Maj. Kenneth Preston then stepped to the podium and said the following words:

"This stone will give soldiers past and present, and those who aspire to wear the uniform of a soldier, the opportunity to reflect on Paul's actions two years ago—actions that saved the lives of 100 of his fellow soldiers. It is because of his dedication that Paul solidified the very core of our Army. On that day, 100 American Soldiers witnessed and learned leadership of extraordinary proportions—leadership that changed and influenced their lives forever.

"Paul was honored with the highest award our nation can bestow a hero. He has become a part of history to his country. For as long as our flag stands, these two hundred acres of sacred ground will cradle our heroes and the memory of Paul's commitment..."

Such kind and honest words from such a great man. Then Birgit, escorted by Sgt. Major Prestin, walked up to the headstone were she placed a lovely red, white and blue wreath before being escorted back to her seat. Then Birgit and the children were escorted back to the stone, where David and his mother lifted off the cloth. Suddenly, David gently placed his tiny little hand on the top of the stone with such a sad expression. Birgit knelt to say a prayer and her tears mixed with the perspiration that had formed on her face. David put his hand on her shoulder as if to comfort her.

I didn't think that the unveiling of the stone would affect me as it did, but the day had been full of such emotional surprises; as I lowered my head I wept. One by one we all walked to the stone to say our good-byes. As Dad knelt by it he seemed to just fold over with grief. My wonderful sister saw this and came and knelt with us to pray.

You know better than most, Paul, that Dad hardly ever shows his emotions and I felt so sorry for him; he had held it all in for so long and today was just too much for all of us. As the family knelt and prayed, we held each other for comfort and I was looking at the gold lettering on the stone and thought, yes, this is the personification of all you deserved for all your life.

I watched as your namesake, Olivia Rae danced around us and seemed to be oblivious of the facts. She was waving a little American flag on a stick and then she placed it gently on the ground by your stone. She is so innocent and sweet. Sadly for her, she is too young and most likely won't remember you; but she will surely know of your love and greatness.

The family returned to our seats one by one and waited for this to be over. The soldier on the hill came into view and raised the bugle that I had not noticed before. As if time had stopped and I was blinded by my tears, he started to play "Taps" and that was all I could handle; right then and there I just wanted God to take me home, too.

I knew at that very moment that I would never be able to go on without you in my life. As if a lightening bolt had cut me in half, my life had been split in two: life with you and life without you. How in this world will I ever go on?

I know that, for me, I will fight this war till the day I die.

I'm Going Home

I'm glad to be going home to my cats and my gardens, to the silence of my nights and the singing birds in the morning. I wonder if any of it will matter or sound or feel the same; probably not.

I will be glad to hide from the world and the prying eyes of the media, with their questions that I don't ever want to answer again. I will get up in the morning, tell myself to breathe and maybe one day I won't have to do that anymore.

Somehow, I'm afraid that's as good as it's ever going to be again…

Closure

My feelings have come together somewhat and as I try to sum up everything that has occurred because of what you did, it's hard for me to realize that I have not died for the loss of you. I guess that God still has a plan for me, after all. I know that I must end this journal but I also know that a new one will begin. I still can't make it through the day without talking to you so, yes, a new journal will start.

As I sit here and look at the pictures of you I have on the wall I can still see my funny little boy with those big blue-green eyes that always said, "I love you, Mom." I will remember that you never forgot my birthday, Mothers day, Christmas or any other holiday.

I'll never forget the laughter you brought into my life, even when—*especially* when—I didn't have anything to laugh about. I'll remember the kindness that you always showed me; the same special brand of kindness that now reverberates in your son, David. Your smile, which always contained sunshine, even on the cloudy days, will still fill me with joy and brighten for all my days to come.

How do I feel about the Medal of Honor? In the end, it's just a pretty blue ribbon with a medal hanging from it that says "Valor." It's cold and unfeeling. The medal is just a medal to me; it can't hug me, or say, "I love you, Mom."

You had so many medals; this one is added to your collection. I do feel that the medal was given to you rightfully. It was given to you for a lifetime of sacrifice, a lifetime of dedication, devotion, and most of all loyalty, not just in your military personage but in everything you did.

For the love you gave to everyone that you ever met, for a lifetime of doing what was right instead of what was just okay. For doing your best in everything you did, for being a righteous and good man. I believe you got this medal for being the kind of father that every child deserves to have in their lives, and for being the son that every mother wants and can be proud of.

As a small boy, as a young man, and as a great soldier you were here for too short a time but in that very short time you blessed us all with your presence. Along the path of your life you touched people in a way that you never even knew about. You taught us all lessons about life and how to live a good one. Because you were here, Paul, the world was a much better place.

You walked quietly among us and left a giant legacy to your family.

How do I sum up this journal?

I will be grateful every day. I will be thankful every day. Why, when I have so much to grieve? Because the Lord is good and has blessed me with your wonderful brother, your two wonderful sisters, grandchildren that make life worth living and put a song in my heart. I have a kind and loving husband, and the Lord gives me what I need for this day. I am blessed.

I will live my life to honor and respect and to do my best in all I do. I will cherish everything that you ever taught me—and are still teaching me. I will miss you everyday but I know I will see you again.

The gold lettering on the headstone that is in Arlington National Cemetery says it all: "His spirit lives forever."

Paul, know this: it lives in all of us.

JOB WELL DONE.

YOU ALWAYS WERE,

MY SON, MY HERO.

BORN A SAPPER…

LIVED A SAPPER…

DIED A SAPPER.

HOOAH! (It's an Army thing!)

THE END…

PAUL RAY SMITH WAS BORN IN EL PASO, TEXAS ON SEPTEMBER 24, 1969.

AT AGE 9, HIS FAMILY MOVED TO THE PALMA CEIA AREA IN SOUTH TAMPA, FLORIDA WERE HE WENT TO PUBLIC SCHOOLS , MAKING AVERAGE GRADES. AS A YOUNG BOY, HE MOST ENJOYED PLAYING FOOTBALL WITH HIS BEST FRIEND AT THE NEIGHBORHOOD CORONA PARK. AS A CORONA COWBOY FOOTBALL PLAYER HE DEVELOPED A SENCE OF TEAM INVOLVMENT. HE LEARNED EARLY IN LIFE HOW TO BE A LEADER AND THE IMPORTANCE OF BEING PART OF THE TEAM. PAUL HAD A LOVE FOR CATS, SKATE BOARDING, RIDING BIKES WITH HIS FRIENDS, AND BEING A JOKER AND PRANKSTER AT TIMES WITH HIS YOUNGER SISTER.

AS A HIGH SCHOOL STUDENT HE DEVELOPED AN INTEREST IN CARPENTRY AND WHILE IN SCHOOL WORKED AS A CARPENTERS ASSISTANT. OTHER INTERESTS WERE OLD CARS, PAINTING FIGURES WITH HIS OLDER BROTHER, RESTORING A DUMB BUGGIE WITH HIS BEST FRIEND, PAUL LOVED TAKING THINGS APART TO SEE HOW THEY WORKED. PAUL WAS A COLLECTOR OF EVERY THING, OTHER WISE KNOWN AS A PACK RAT. COLLECTIONS INCLUDED, ANY THING FROM THE SEA, ANY STRANGE ROCK , MARBELS, OR ANYTHING ELSE THAT SEEMED UNUSUAL. AS A YOUNG MAN, PAUL ALREADY SEEMED TO KNOW WERE HE WAS GOING IN LIFE BECAUSE ANY TIME SOMEONE WOULD ASK HIM WHAT HE WANTED TO DO AS AN ADULT, HE SIMPLY SAID, (I WANT TO BE A SOLDIIER , GET MARRIED AND HAVE BABYS.)

UPON GRADUATING IN 1988 FROM TAMPA BAY VO TECH, HE JOINED THE MILITARY AND WENT TO FORT LENINWOOD MO. FOR BOOT CAMP. GRADUATING BOOT CAMP WAS THE BEGINNING OF A LIFE LONG DREAM. . ASSIGNMENTS IN GERMANY, MEETING AND MARRIEING HIS LOVELY WIFE, HAVING TWO BEAUTIFUL CHILDREN AND DOING WHAT HE WAS BORN TO DO, LEAD.

IN HIS TRAVELS, HE NEVER FORGOT HOW IMPORTANT FAMILY WAS AND OFTEN TOOK LEAVE TO VISIT.

HE WAS AFFECTIONATE, LOYAL, DEDICATED AND WISE. HE WAS STRONG IN VALUES AND TENDER IN HEART WITH AN ENGAGING SMILE THAT WAS LIKE A TRADE MARK..

PAULS LOVE OF FAMILY, COUNTRY, AND FREEDOM WAS THE REASON!
EVERY DAY HE LIVED LIFE TO THE FULLEST AND ALWAYS TRIED TO DO BETTER THAN YESTERDAY. HE SAW THE GOOD IN EVERY LIFE THAT HE TOUCHED, AND TRIED TO HELP ANY ONE THAT NEEDED HIM.

IN HIS FOURTEEN-YEAR CAREER, HE GAVE HIS ALL TO HIS FAMILY, TO HIS COUNTRY, AND , HE GAVE THE ULTIMATE FOR FREEDOM.

HOOAH.

About the author

She is a wife...a mother...a homemaker

Throughout her years of motherhood balancing jobs, being a single parent trying to keep her sanity in a fast paced world that often times left her numb and exhausted. Some times to exhausted to stop and smell the roses or focus in on much of any thing. Some were between jobs, housekeeping and trying to keep up with four active children she used writing as an outlet most of her life. Keeping journals to see were she had been and to help guide her future with fewer mistakes.

Writing short stories and poetry from early motherhood her greatest inspiration for these works has come mostly from her children. Other works have come from places she has lived and experiences out of her own life.

She has kept her writings on a computer and mostly to herself.... Until now.

In 2003 she and her husband of twenty years lost their beloved youngest son in the Iraq war. Paul Ray was only 33 years old...in the prime of his life. He had dedicated his life to family and career, fourteen years in the United States Army. He left behind a wife, two children, two sisters, and a brother. He left behind a mother with a broken heart. He left behind an emptiness that no great legacy could ever fill.

In today's world it is easy for parents to be so wrapped up in the act of living that they some times can't see the really important things in their lives. They don't seem to mind that our children have made heroes out of baseball players, they put football giants on pedestals to be admired and in general have worship complexes toward movie stars and rock performers. This is a journal that she hopes will help children to know and learn about what it takes to be a real hero.

This is an intimate look into the life of a mother's two-year grief journal to finding closure with her beloved son's death. She will share with you the rage, anger, sorrow, and tears that she felt on her journey. She would like this journal to help other parents that are struggling with a lose of a loved one, She states "we must remember that our lives have been altered for all times but it has not ended, we must go on."

JP and her husband share their home in south Florida with three cats that own the house and allow them to live there also. They have lived in Florida for twenty-five years and consider themselves natives.

With the loss of her son, JP has realized the cost of her procrastination and although this is her first publication she vows that it won't be her last.

978-0-595-67457-2
0-595-67457-7

Printed in the United States
42953LVS00007B/1-51